# Embracing Soul Care

# Embracing Soul Care

## Making Space for What Matters Most

STEPHEN W. SMITH

Kregel
Publications

**Library of Congress Cataloging-in-Publication Data**
Smith, Stephen W.
  Embracing soul care : making space for what matters most / by Stephen W. Smith.
    p.  cm.
  1. Spiritual formation. I. Title.
BV4501.3.S6565    2006
248.—dc22                                        2006010338

ISBN 0-8254-3670-2

Printed in the United States of America

06 07 08 09 10 / 5 4 3 2 1

For Gwen Harding Smith

You have given to me what my soul has always yearned for:
the touch of your soul next to mine;
the presence lingering with me while we move on and through;
ears larger than my own to listen to the Greater Voice;
curiosity to explore the unseen and the sacred;
courage to face the truth, and grace . . . marvelous grace
to try again and again.
In you, I have found love. Your love is what
I need and want.

Thank you for caring for my broken soul!

# Contents

PART 11: SOUL COMPANIONS: FRIENDSHIP ON THE JOURNEY

PART 12: SOUL SIGNIFICANCE: FINDING MEANING AND LOOKING AHEAD

PART 13: SOUL CELEBRATIONS: MARKING THE EVENTS OF THE SOUL

# Foreword

*I*f you're like me, when you read a spiritual-growth book you want to be assured of the author's authenticity. Does this person practice what he or she writes? Does the author understand your life, your questions, even your doubts and mistakes? If you met the author in person, would his or her lifestyle match the claims of the book?

For Stephen W. Smith, the answer to all these questions is yes. He's devoted his life and ministry to soul care. His personal library brims with books on the subject, and he spends thoughtful time with God. He's led group retreats and intensive individual spiritual explorations to help Christians grow their souls. But Steve is also the first to tell you that he's a spiritual struggler. He has forged his own soul care through failure, frustration, and a desperate desire to change self-destructive patterns. He'll also say that, through soul care, he's moved closer to a loving God, who has comforted, healed, and guided him to a more satisfying life. Steve believes soul care is not just the latest hot topic but an essential, lifelong practice for every Christian.

Let me tell you how true soul care entered Steve's life.

At thirty-seven years old, Steve served as the senior pastor of the largest church in Durham, North Carolina. He preached three Sunday morning services, oversaw a staff of seventeen, conducted weddings and funerals, counseled people, and attended a variety of meetings scattered through the week. His ministry thrived, but that left little time for family life and the private care of his own soul.

"It all looked successful on the outside," Steve recalls, "but on the inside, I was imploding."

Several years into this pastorate, Steve invited me to speak at his church on a Sunday morning. I spoke about the five love languages that people use to express their love to one another. These "languages" are words of affirmation, quality time, gifts, acts of service, and physical touch. All of these actions figure into loving relationships, but each of us possesses a primary love language—a specific action that, when directed toward us, makes us feel loved. If, for example, your love language is gifts, you feel loved when a spouse, family member, or friend gives you a present.

After the third service that Sunday morning, Steve rushed home to eat lunch with his wife and four young sons, before a 2:30 PM meeting with the church's deacons. As Steve explains it, he felt compelled to put in "Dad time" before his next ministry obligation. At the table, he asked his oldest son, then in the fifth grade, about the morning's sermon on love languages.

"Did you like the sermon, Blake?"

"Yes, Dad, I loved it."

"Did you understand the love languages?"

"Yes, I did."

"What's your love language, Blake?"

"Dad, my love language is quality time, and you never give me any."

Steve felt stunned, speechless. "My soul had been filleted open," he explains. "I realized that I'd been sacrificing my son for the sake of my career." He left the house in remorse and, a short time later, resigned his pastorate.

Most of us would immediately look for another job, but Steve took six months to get counseling, reformat his life, and learn to care for his soul. Three Christian men acted as his soul companions, supporting him, pointing him toward a deeper relationship with God, and helping him break an addiction to work and success. Steve also reshaped his relationship with his wife and children, spending more time with them and caring about their needs.

"I had preached that the soul needs to be saved, but I didn't know what to do with it after that," admits Steve. "I'd hated books about soul care. They meant slowing down and measuring myself by something other than church-growth figures and my salary. Those books asked me to look inside, to pay attention to my soul, and to find my identity in God."

But eventually, to save his life, that's what Steve did.

Those six months paid off. Steve and his wife, Gwen, grounded themselves in soul care, and now they compassionately help Christians nurture their relationships with God. Through their ministry, The Potter's Inn, they conduct retreats, write books, counsel seekers, and offer soul care. The Smiths want people to grasp their belovedness to God and understand that he alone can heal and refuel their souls. Much of what they believe about soul care has been distilled into the daily devotional you hold in your hands. In *Embracing Soul Care,* Steve provides a user-friendly guide to caring for the spiritual person within you. The thirteen sections invite you to walk around your soul, look at it from different perspectives, and learn how to deepen your walk with the heavenly Father.

Steve often quotes these Bible verses to describe what soul care has done for him: "Now I'm glad . . . that you were jarred into turning things around. You let the distress bring you to God, not drive you from him. The result was all gain, no loss. . . . You're more alive, more concerned, more sensitive, more reverent, more human, more passionate, more responsible. Looked at from any angle, you've come out of this with purity of heart" (2 Cor. 7:9, 11 MSG).

With this practical guide you, too, can discover the life-changing joy of soul care.

—GARY D. CHAPMAN

Author, *The Five Love Languages*

# Preface

The work of art depicted on the cover of this book is *Poplars,* by Claude Monet. The way of looking at life expressed by the artistic reflections of impressionism converges with the important subject of this book to allow an insight into the dynamics of our experience with God.

*Impressionism* is a term given to a movement of art that developed in Paris among a group of artists who wanted to break with the staid conventions of painting in the mid-1800s. This phenomenon developed under the brush strokes of a number of innovators, but none were more important than Claude Monet. These artists sought to "do" art in a whole new way.

What began with a vision in Monet's own heart unfolded to become a style revolution that is still popular and influential. Monet's artistic colleagues in early impressionism included Camille Pisarro, Pierre-Auguste Renoir, Edgar Degas, Edouard Manet, and Alfred Sisley. Together, they forged a new way of seeing life, and they interpreted what they saw with oil on canvas.

Monet captured reality by emphasizing degrees and shades of light, by using various new brush strokes, and by painting ordinary subjects and landscapes in extraordinary ways. He used unusual perspectives to help the observer capture something that could not be seen in physical reality. His own impressions of what he saw were unleashed on canvas. Monet even provided the name for this movement. In 1873, he painted the harbor at Le Havre in France. When asked what the painting should be called, Monet said, "Put 'Impression.'"[1] Thus, this great art movement got its name of impressionism.

The distinguishing brush strokes of Monet offered suggestions— or impressions—of a reality that people could only see by pondering with the imagination instead of only the eyes. Impressionist art is something to be pondered.

Impressionist painting and the journey I call soul care have much in common. Both follow a path that is nonlinear in development. Soul care, like impressionism, is not a cookie-cutter, step-by-step approach. Soul care, like impressionism, is fluid, open, and offers multiple ways of looking at the same thing. Both require some degree of creativity and abstract thinking.

The soul is a deep, spiritual reality that is hard to define. The soul is a mystery and can best be understood by looking at it, as Monet looked at the poplars he painted, from different angles and perspectives. People of all ages, religions, and times have sought, though, to put the soul in a box so that we can have a better understanding when we speak of the soul. But the soul cannot be put in a box, as you will discover in this book.

I chose *Poplars* because Monet invested himself in this stand of poplar trees near his home. He was so impressed with them that he bought the land on which the trees stood. By purchasing the trees, he saved them from being cut for lumber. The artist painted those trees twenty-three times, showing them in different seasons, times of the day, and with varying degrees of detail. The trees no longer stand, but the paintings survive, leaving something that might be called "soulish" for us to consider.

The composition of *Poplars* is also suggestive. Look closely at the trees. The row of trees develops in a curve, rather than a straight line. The curve creates movement and progression for the eye, just as movement and progression can be seen in the journey of the soul. The trees in the painting are all similar, yet each is different. The trees are separated from one another by a comfortable space, just as we need separateness for individuality. Yet we are called to community. The line of trees leads the eye around that bend and into the distance, as if inviting the viewer to follow. God invites us beyond the bend in the path, to discover what lies within a well-cared-for soul.

Something deeper lies within the painting. He painted the scene from many perspectives, and under many conditions. He spent time, personal effort, soul, and material resources to interpret what he saw. Soul care works in much the same way, requiring attention over time from different perspectives, and under changing conditions. Each of us must make an investment in the care of our souls. As Jesus said, "What good will it be for a man if he gains the whole world, yet forfeits his soul? Or what can a man give in exchange for his soul?" (Matt. 16:26). Jesus elevated the soul's importance, showing that it was of incomparable value. Caring for the soul should be our highest priority. It's what matters most. We can gain much, but if we lose our souls in the process, what good is that gain?

As we continue the journey of soul care, let us begin with curiosity and thirst. For some, this will be a new sort of journey. For others, it will be another "impression" perspective regarding how to practice care of the soul. Whether novice or experienced, the important thing is to do soul care.

# Acknowledgments

*M*y own soul has been deeply cared for by some amazing saints—some who still walk this earth and others now in heaven. I am fortunate to have been graced in life with people who introduced me to the care of my own soul. I'm sure this is because God knew I would need such help in learning.

My primary soul-care mentor is my wife, Gwen. Since 1980, she has been both companion and pastor to my own soul, living and "doing" soul care as no one else I have ever met. My sons have now matured beyond what I have written about them here. Blake, Jordan, Cameron, and Leighton have given to me forgiveness and unconditional love.

Dallas Willard, Glenn Hinson, Larry Crabb, Michael Cusick, Brent Curtis, Ken Gire, and David Benner helped me find the language by which to express words that I knew must exist. I am indebted to these men and others for teaching, books, conversations, and encouragement.

My primary soulful advocates are the men and women who believe in the ministry of the Potter's Inn. It takes the support of many to make this work possible. Gwen and I stand upon strong shoulders in offering the soul-care message, and we never stand alone. I especially thank Michael and Hallie Doyle, Ray and Lynn Walkowski, and Paul and Paula Meredith for both standing with us in this ministry and being wonderful soul care practitioners.

Special thanks to Judith Couchman, Gloria Smith Schwartz, Leslie Meredith, and Paul Ingram for artistic help in coaching, editing, and challenging me to produce these written words. Heartfelt thanks also go to Dennis Hillman at Kregel Publications, who believed in this book, and Gary Foster, who nurtured this vision like a baby and has walked with me to its birth.

Special people were in my life at significant times, giving help that I didn't always want or feel I needed. Those who gave soul care to save me from imploding and scattering carnage everywhere include Ed Thain, Steve Metcalf, Paula Rinehart, Joanne Hodgson, Susan Jones, Chuck Millsaps, Jack and Jane Wood, Alma Lee, Sue Northcutt, Tim Oakley, Jason Krusiewicz, Rick Campbell, and Craig Glass.

This book is dedicated to the men and women who go wherever God sends them to share the hope of the gospel. Some call them missionaries. I call them heroes. I hope this book gives back a little to those who have given so much.

—STEPHEN W. SMITH
Potter's Inn at Aspen Ridge
March 2006

# Introduction

*F*or more than a half century, I've been searching for something—how to care for my soul. For much of that time, I was oblivious to what I was really searching for. Like the prodigal, I was on a hunt for something more. Some of this search, though, has been more like a journey—more intentional. My hunt became a journey of exploring my soul and God's love for me.

Finding one's self and finding Jesus brings a care of the soul that every person needs. Without discovering my own soul and without Jesus, I'd still be the prodigal in the pig sty, rooting for something that would fill my soul. Along the way, two words seemed to converge in my life, *soul* and *care*. We can profit by thinking of *soul care* as God and other Christian thinkers through the ages have presented it—a single-minded priority in our spiritual growth.

The educational pursuits of theology and philosophy show the mystery and let us in on the debates regarding the soul. Great art, wonderful music, and delicious food all make us aware that the soul is larger, deeper, and more important than we imagined. But not until I became aware that something inside of me was broken and needing to be fixed did I begin a deeper part of my journey to understand how to care for my soul. In this book, I share my search for soul care and offer you ways to explore caring for your own soul.

For me, soul care has been a pilgrimage. I have several diplomas to remind me that I know certain things, but no diploma gave me what I need most in life. No job did either, nor did any person, higher income level, or shiny new car. The acquiring of information, important positions in work, or connections with people who "had it together," did not change me. Was there anything or anyone to assuage my soulful longings?

Rather than care for my soul, I long tried to fill myself through effort and socially acceptable achievements. I thought that would give my soul what it needed. I performed because I learned early in life that if I performed well, I would be given what I sought for most.

Then, through some difficult experiences I learned that my soul is not an "it." My soul is me—the real me. Your soul is the real you. That seems such an obvious thing to say, but it isn't always wrong to state the obvious. Sometimes we lose our way.

I didn't know how important I really was to God, so I didn't hold myself to be very important. I didn't value what God valued. I didn't hold holy what God considers holy. I moved to the cadence of performance and success. Like a hamster, I got on a wheel and ran and ran and ran. During part of this time I pastored churches and herded members as if they were cattle rather than shepherding them as sacred souls. My soul was driven, until the shaft that held up my hamster wheel snapped. Wreckage flew everywhere as my soul collapsed in upon itself. Implosions are very messy.

I realized then that unless I actually "did" what matters most, I would keep imploding, ruining my life and the lives of those I loved. This journey of exploring what matters most in life is the journey of soul care. I'm still on this journey. I have not arrived. Fortunately, the strong and loving hands of the divine Potter are still busy at the task. This book is a guide to exploring and caring for your soul as it is shaped in those hands. It is a pilgrimage inside to the real you.

Author and professor Daniel Taylor has pointed out that "the greatest danger of pilgrimage, always, is the temptation to live off someone else's experience and transcendence."[1] I have made that mistake—fascinated by other people's stories of spiritual adventure but never quite trying to take my own journey. So this book is not about my journey; it is for *your* journey, to allow you to have your own experiences and encounters with your very true God. To make this a more inward experience, each chapter offers several questions to ponder and work through. By working through the questions, you'll work your way deeper, toward the wonder and the mystery of you and the Christ who resides in you.

Soul care takes time to learn. The more you practice, the better you get at it. Perhaps you'll discover in this book a certain rhythm for that care, an "unforced rhythm of grace," as Eugene Peterson calls it.[2] You may think of better questions than I pose. Whatever the questions, ponder them and live them. Ponder them and use those insights to catch a glimpse of the real you and our very real God.

Life is fragile. It's time for soul care. The Psalmist says, "When anxiety was great within me, your consolation brought joy to my soul" (Ps. 94:19). This verse alone should offer hope in the midst of fragile times, both within our own souls and in this world in which we live.

May you find the joy of the soul care journey.

—STEPHEN W. SMITH
Potter's Inn at Aspen Ridge

## PART 1

# SOUL CARE

*Meeting the Needs of
the Inner Person*

# Taking the Time

The best time to plant a tree is twenty years ago. The second best time is now.

AFRICAN PROVERB

What could you ever trade your soul for?

MATTHEW 16:26 MSG

*A* friend inherited a collection of old windup watches from her mother. Her mother complained that after she wore each timepiece for a few months, it stopped working. Something in her body chemistry made it stop, but instead of taking a watch to a shop for repair, she banished it to her jewelry box and purchased another. The jewelry box turned into a watch dump—and the woman still couldn't find a watch that kept on ticking.

Old watches and clocks need regular maintenance so they don't end up at the timepiece cemetery. The traditional mechanical clocks run because of an intricate set of gears and wheels. One wheel interlocks with another to move the hands through the minutes and hours. The simple face of a watch conceals an amazing interconnected process.

The soul of a human being can be compared to that mechanical clock. The soul is that part of a person that lies behind the face at the mechanism's core. The soul integrates all the parts of a person's life—the people, places, events, thoughts, and feelings. The soul, then, is the center of who we are, past, present, and future. Our soul holds our hopes, longings, and desires, our passions, gifts, and individuality.

As an old clock needs the attention of a watchmaker, the soul needs care. An old clock cannot work indefinitely without maintenance. Digital clocks seem to practically run themselves, but humans are not so modernized. Our hearts, minds, and bodies require care, or we run down.

Soul care helps maintain the interconnectedness of the mind, body, heart, and soul and keeps us spiritually alive. Nothing substitutes for making the soul a priority. Jesus asked, "What could you ever trade your soul for?" (Matt. 16:26 MSG). The same question that Jesus posed to his followers years ago still haunts our fast-paced world.

A man recently told me he suffered from "hamster-wheel syndrome. I move as fast as I can through each day yet never feel I'm making any real progress. I'm tired, breathless, and lonely. I don't know how to get off of the spinning hamster wheel." This friend needs time for inner maintenance, rest, and repair. We all do.

Soul care begins with time. But that doesn't mean we have to tear apart our "insides" for weeks of repair and downtime. We can begin the soul's care with small time commitments. By tinkering here, cleaning and polishing there, we refurbish the soul. Some may need to "get away from it all" for a major overhaul, but for most of us, day-by-day maintenance will add up to soul care. Now is the time to begin.

## Your Soul Care

1. If you were a windup watch, what condition would you be in today?
2. What maintenance or repair would you need?
3. What level of time commitment are you ready to make for refurbishing your soul?

# 2

# Soul Care 101

The desperate need today is not for a greater number of
intelligent people, or gifted people, but for deep people.

RICHARD FOSTER

The LORD is my shepherd.
I shall not want. . . .
He restores my soul.

PSALM 23:1, 3 NKJV

So what, exactly, is soul care? It is living soulfully. *Soulful* means
"full of feeling or emotion." But I'd like to redefine *soulful* to fit
soul care: "With the nurturing of the soul in mind."

Soul care takes us past the immediate and physical to what is truly
important. It figures out what truly matters in life and then realigns
the self to those higher priorities. Focusing on the truly important
dimension of life, we realize that soul development requires a lifelong process of examining spiritual reality. Soul care involves relationships, personal spiritual growth, inner healing and change, rest
and rejuvenation, and living with heaven in mind. It slows down the
frenetic lifestyle to make time for the soul.

In contrast, much of our generation insists upon instant gratifica-
tion. Many live with myopic vision focused on the immediate, the
money, and the allure of success. And we want it now. This value
system gives only empty, hollow feelings of superficial success, stealing any sense of real purpose. Our goals are limited to today at the
expense of the ultimate. We sacrifice the core of who we are to chase
passing interests. We don't know how to serve others.

People who live from their soul regularly make changes that move toward authentic transformation, not pseudochange.[1] They want what God wants for them. They embrace the best as truly the best and try not to settle for less. They evolve into "deep people" who live beyond appointments and cell phones. They might make appointments for prayer and communion with God or notes to remind themselves to serve others or call someone for spiritual support. They know that they are not alone. They know that they are not self-made.

Shallow people hit dead ends. They go it alone, having no substance to hold them up. The wind can blow them away like straw. They faint and quit. Sometimes they become cynical about their lives and faith. They ask, "Why am I here?"

Tending your soul stretches you to seek what really matters. You are caring for a person God cares for—you. Do you think it selfish to care for your own soul? Do you consider it a luxury? If so, consider that soul care leads us into more fulfilling relationships, purposeful work, and a sense that God is with us. Plumbers, teachers, business leaders, homemakers, or merchants begin to look upon work as a calling. We perform our duties soulfully.

Exploring the value, worth, and dimensions of the soul ventures inside, reflects on how to practice soul care, and helps us describe the states inside. Can we find God's profound and unconditional love? Might we discover what gives us joy and makes us feel more alive?

Still, soul care isn't a cookie-cutter process. God makes each human as a unique individual. We discover satisfaction as we shape our spiritual practices in ways that nourish and restore our individual souls. Then we can reemerge into the world to passionately pursue our calling, as we love and support others on their paths.

## Your Soul Care

1. What does it mean to practice soul care?
2. What makes you feel physically and spiritually alive?
3. Can you name three things that help you feel restored?

# 3

# The Inner Longing

The meaning of earthly existence is not, as we have grown
used to thinking, in prosperity, but in the development
of the soul.

ALEKSANDR SOLZHENITSYN

What good will it be for a man if he gains the whole
world, yet forfeits his soul?

MATTHEW 16:26

*J*esus asked the provocative question, "What good will it be for
a man if he gains the whole world, yet forfeits his soul?" (Matt.
16:26). His question evaluates the trajectory of our life. Gaining the
whole world has the trappings of success. Forfeiting the soul looks
from the inside like lingering emptiness, purposelessness, and futil-
ity. Looking at these prospects, we need to ask, "What am I *losing* by
all of the *gaining* I am doing?"

Thomas Moore, a psychologist and author, said that the great
malady of this time in Western history is the "loss of soul."[1] Without
soul, we base our lives on doing, getting, achieving, and performing.
Our egos protest when someone challenges these actions. Regardless
of the ego's opinions, old ideas will be challenged as we begin to look
for a true source of authenticity.

Whether we are prodding quietly or knocked to our knees, our
souls remind us of the "more" that we crave. The sacred hunger we
feel is not satisfied by bread alone. Rather, God is at the window of
the soul, looking in. "The LORD does not look at the things man
looks at. Man looks at the outward appearance, but the LORD looks

at the heart" (1 Sam. 16:7). God tells us, *Look inside. That's what matters.*

Soul care integrates all of a person, beginning with the inner being. Only God can peer into a soul to see perfectly what we cannot see. He says, "I the LORD search the heart and examine the mind" (Jer. 17:10a). Deep inside are desires, passions, longings, regrets, motives, and intuitions about God, family, work, and other dimensions of life. All is revealed to him.

In Matthew 16, Jesus challenges us to explore our inner geography. He invites us to wake up and be curious about the sacred space inside. As a consequence, we, too, see through the windows of our souls to the hunger that lies beneath the surface. We begin to feed that magnificent longing by a relationship with the Divine.

As Christians, we are taught that Jesus lives within us. That's an easy statement to make, but it is still a mystery. The apostle Paul tells us, "The mystery in a nutshell is just this: Christ is in you, therefore you can look forward to sharing in God's glory" (Col. 1:27 MSG). And knowing that Jesus dwells inside arouses our longing that Jesus will embrace our souls.

Thomas Moore reminds us, "When the soul is neglected, it doesn't just go away; it appears symptomatically in obsessions, addictions, violence, and loss of meaning."[2] Can we relate to these symptoms? Do we have the willingness to opt for life, love, and soul wisdom?

*Your Soul Care*

1. Which Scripture in this reading resonates with you most? How?
2. What are other reasons soul care matters?
3. Do your inner longings point to God?

# The Ancient Path

Physician of my sin-sick soul,
To thee I bring my case;
My raging malady control,
And heal me by thy grace.

JOHN NEWTON

It is not the healthy who need a doctor, but the sick. I have not come to call the righteous, but sinners.

MARK 2:17

Our family was taking a trip, when I suddenly slammed on the brakes. One of our children had cried out in agony, "I'm going to throw up," resulting in an emergency evacuation from the car. Earlier in the day, we'd gone to an amusement park. The rides, cotton candy, soft drinks, and who knows what else all contributed to the cry that every parent fears—especially when going sixty-five miles per hour down the interstate. I stopped the car in time, and after my son had brought up what had earlier gone down, he climbed back into the car, announcing, "I feel good all over now." What a way to feel better.

Soul care is not a new invention or a fad. It's been around, in fact, as long as there have been empty souls. Throughout time and in every religion people have been trying to care for their souls in many ways. Soul care is a tried-and-true journey, as ancient and natural as life itself.

Jewish prophets, wise leaders, and rabbis sought to care for souls in their teaching and shepherding ministries. Jesus referred to himself as the Good Shepherd, offering his staff and arms as a protective haven. In the early church, God endowed people with spiritual gifts to lead and love their spiritual flocks and tend their souls. Paul wrote inspiring letters to fledgling churches, and believers tended to the needs of one another to edify the soul.

Disease in the body can be treated by medical practitioners. But the *dis-ease* of our souls needs something more. The soul experiences dis-ease through stress, moral failure, broken relationships, pressures within and without, and addictions. The purpose of healing our souls is not to build a temple inside in which to sit and contemplate—to "navel gaze" as some call it. Instead, as our souls heal, we live as never before. This is part of the abundant life that Jesus promises us (see John 10:10). It's not all future. Abundance of life can be realized now.

From Genesis to the Revelation, a passionate God does whatever it takes to care for his people's souls. Even now, nothing will hold him back from helping us heal, grow, and fulfill our purpose, because untended, the soul will not thrive. First through God's prophets, then through his Son, and now through his people, soul care awaits us.

We were made with a yearning for God, a divine discontent. From ancient times, Christians have known this and tended to their souls and the souls of others. Soul care is not a job just for professional therapists, pastors, and spiritual directors, valuable though they may be. Our mission as ordinary men and women of God is to love each other deeply—from the heart. Empowered with gifts, talents, and abilities, we are all called to enter into a mutual and reciprocal relationship in which care, love, and grace are freely exchanged among us. Fifty-four times the New Testament encourages us to do so, through commands known as the "one another passages." We're encouraged to love one another (John 13:34); build up one another (1 Thess. 5:11); and forgive one another (Eph. 4:32). Through soul care, we live the gospel message.

Soul care was taught by the prophets, modeled by Jesus, and practiced by early Christians. Now we are reclaiming what is good for the soul so that we can thrive. When we follow the ancient path, we can be sure we are following a path that many pilgrims have walked.

## Your Soul Care

1. Why do you think God designed souls to need care?
2. In what ways does your soul need care?
3. What would thriving look like in your soul?

# 5

# The Heart of the Matter

A life without heart is not worth living. For out of this
wellspring of our soul flow all true caring and all meaningful work, all real worship and all sacrifice.

BRENT CURTIS AND JOHN ELDREDGE

Above all else, guard your heart,
for it is the wellspring of life.

PROVERBS 4:23

*I*n our misunderstanding, a friend and I found ourselves both
frustrated. We were not communicating because we were talking
around the issue instead of getting it out in the open. "Steve, just
get to the heart of the matter," he finally admonished. This gave me
permission to candidly share what I was feeling. I felt safe with this
friend. I could speak from my heart, knowing that he would understand, even if he did not agree.

The metaphor of the human heart as the center of our being is one
of the oldest and most compelling in human history. The heart-as-
center represents not the blood-pumping muscle but the core of who
we are as individuals distinct from other life-forms. Our hearts bear
the DNA of God. Sometimes we use the word *heart* when what we
are really referring to is the *soul*. The heart is where our will meets
our desire, passion, love, and awe. The soul embodies all of this and
more.

The heart-as-center metaphor, though, is one of the most frequently and easily understood expressions. In everyday vernacular,
*heart* expresses vulnerability. It's often said, "Oh, why don't you have

a heart?" or "You should take this to heart," or "This person is just hard-hearted." Expressions like these have clear meaning.

I have four sons. When my wife and I watch them compete in sports, we often hear people comment, "Wow, they really played with all their heart!" I know what they mean. My boys gave their best effort, even if their team lost. Some friends gave a gift to my wife and me explaining, "This is from our heart." We understood, and their gift is doubly cherished.

The Bible uses the concept of the heart to describe where the real relationship with God occurs. The hymn writer Emily Elliott wrote, "Oh come to my heart, Lord Jesus, there is room in my heart for you."[1] In expressing this petition to Jesus, Elliott pleads for God's presence and invites Jesus to reside inside her heart.

When God was searching for a new leader, a new and noble king, we're told "the LORD has sought out a man after his own heart" (1 Sam. 13:14). God wanted the new leader to possess a heart like his heavenly Father. What a bold request by God. This leader's heart would distinguish him from his tribe. David, the greatest king in Jewish history, united his country as no other ruler in Israel or Judah was able.

The heart and soul of a person matters to God. As the inner teacher in our hearts, the Lord reminds us that we are not taking the journey to soul care alone. God has always walked with us, guided us, and loved us—from his heart.

### Your Soul Care

1. Why are "heart" and "soul" closely related concepts?
2. Why is your heart so valuable to God?
3. When God looks at your heart, what do you envision that he sees?

# 6

# The Art of Curiosity

I became a detective of divinity, collecting evidence
of God's genius and admiring the traces left for me to
follow.

BARBARA BROWN TAYLOR

"Amazing!" Moses said to himself. "Why isn't that bush
burning up? I must go over to see this."
   When the LORD saw that he had caught Moses' attention, God called to him from the bush, "Moses! Moses!"
   "Here I am!" Moses replied.

EXODUS 3:3–4 NLT

*O*ne of my friends describes her three-year-old niece as a "world-
class detective."
   "Nothing gets by her," says her aunt. "She notices everything—
from the yellow markings on a tiny finch in the yard to a piece of lint
on the living room carpet. Her observations, curiosity, and questions astound me. When we're together, she slows me down. I notice
and appreciate things I'd usually let slip by. It's wonderful to be this
curious, to ask questions about the world."
   As we grow older, we tend to lose this innocent wonder. Yet curiosity is integral to soul care. Curiosity invites us to wonder, "What
is God up to in my life? What is he doing in the world?" A curious
soul seeks to know God and appreciates his ways. To reclaim our
curiosity, we simply become more like a child, which is something
Jesus told us to do. He said, "Whoever becomes simple and elemen-
tal again, like this child, will rank high in God's kingdom" (Matt.

18:4 MSG). Curiosity explores what lies beneath the surface and asks questions. It assists our souls in fully experiencing God's presence. We can also follow the example of Moses. Exodus 3 tells the fascinating story of the period when Moses lived in obscurity in the wilderness. As Moses tended a flock, a bush in flames caught his eye. So he approached the bush, driven by curiosity. He explored. He entered the experience. He met God in the burning bush and emerged a changed man. As Moses turned aside with curiosity, we see that God spoke to him at that precise moment.

It's important to note that Moses was not on a spiritual retreat or pilgrimage. God revealed himself to Moses on an ordinary workday. Spiritual encounters with God don't need to be preplanned. He is, after all, always with us. Opening our spiritual eyes and ears—in nature, the workplace, at home, in the shopping center, at a sports event—simply means increasing our awareness of God's presence. In this regard, we become detectives of divinity, drawing closer to God and watching his movement in the world. As a result, we feel his stirrings.

Scriptures encourage us to become detectives of divinity. The psalmist says "Taste and see that the LORD is good" (Ps. 34:8). Jesus calls us to *consider* the lily (Matt. 6:26), *observe* the birds of the air (v. 26), *listen* to the sound of the wind (John 3:8), *look* at the foxes (Matt. 8:20). Such things initiate a holy curiosity about the kingdom of God. Curiosity becomes a sacred invitation to experience God.

So go ahead. Accept the invitation. Be curious—and be ready to meet God.

## Your Soul Care

1. What are you curious about in relationship to God?
2. What robs you of holy curiosity?
3. How can you practice more spiritual curiosity?

## 7

# Help Yourself First

A humble understanding of yourself is a surer way to
God than a profound searching after knowledge.

THOMAS À KEMPIS

And let me live whole and holy, soul and body,
so I can always walk with my head held high.

PSALM 119:80 MSG

The flight attendant on the airplane was busy with flight preparations. Exhausted and numb after meetings, I fastened my seatbelt
for the flight home. After the cabin door closed, the attendant began the typical safety announcements. But this time, for whatever
reason, I listened more closely. She said, "In the unlikely event of a
sudden loss of pressure, oxygen masks will automatically drop. Place
the mask on yourself first, and then help a child or the person next
to you."

The instruction, "Place the mask on yourself first" knocked me
out of my daze. Didn't it sound selfish to breathe before you helped
another person take a breath? On the trip home I applied her words
to life situations. It is alarming how often leaders crash and burn, as
if driven into the flame like a moth seeking light. But burnout is also
the hazard of parents, medical practitioners, counselors, and anyone
who cares for the needs of others.

Many of us in the helping professions don't know when to let
ourselves breathe first. Teachers, preachers, doctors, nurses, social
workers, and missionaries tend to defy the laws of oxygen. However
we're wired, we want to see other people breathe so badly that we

neglect our own air, falsely assuming that we'll take a breath when it's needed. The result is incredible stress, compassion fatigue, and emotional exhaustion. And while we offer our best to our clients, parishioners, needy friends, or students, we give leftovers to those we love most—our family members.

How does a person who wants so badly to help others get the help to breathe first? First, we can remember that no human is the Messiah. No human can give what only God gives. A daily confession of our need for the Messiah helps. We also can learn to care for our souls— making this a priority—before tending to the souls of others.

The old *JOY* acronym that Christians have been taught is *J*-esus, *O*-thers, *Y*-ou. Always yourself last. What this doesn't take into account is that Jesus lives in the soul of every Christian. Jesus is in us. By taking care of the soul, we honor the Christ who dwells within. We honor him first by taking care of ourselves.

## *Your Soul Care*

1. Does it seem self-centered to talk about taking care of your soul first?
2. How can you begin taking care of your soul first?
3. How will taking care of your soul first affect others?

# PART 2

# SOUL IDENTITY

*Embracing Who God Created You to Be*

# The Beloved

Self-rejection contradicts the sacred voice that calls us
the Beloved.

HENRI NOUWEN

Jesus knew that the Father had put all things under his
power, and that he had come from God and was returning to God.

JOHN 13:3

*R*ecently a friend described the deepest wound of his life. He'd received it from his mother when he was a boy. A product of humble origins in West Texas, his family was riddled with alcoholism
and emotional and sexual abuses. One day in his formative years, his
mother spoke the piercing words that for years caused a hemorrhage
in his heart. In a drunken outburst, she screamed, "You're nothin'
but white trash. Don't ever forget it." Now in his forties, my friend
is desperate to stop his bleeding heart, to believe that his mother's
haunting pronouncement was and is a lie.

We do not see ourselves as God views us. It takes a lifetime to
even begin to realize who we really are in God's eyes. Judges 6 tells
of Gideon's struggle with his identity. The angel of the Lord said to
Gideon, "The LORD is with you, mighty warrior" (v. 12). Gideon knew
he was not a mighty warrior. He had not done anything outstanding.
Yet this pronouncement identifies the Gideon God made him to be.
At first he resisted this noble status, arguing with the angel: "How
can I save Israel? . . . My clan is the weakest . . . I am the least . . ." (v.
15). Gideon does not accept his true identity. The announcement of

Gideon's identity didn't sink in, but as his life unfolded, he lived out his "mighty warrior" name. Gideon moved forward in courageous faith, certain that God accompanied him. Knowing God's view of him, Gideon became a mighty warrior.

Poor self-worth can harm the spiritual life. Many of us struggle with who we are in Christ and our identity as God's beloved.[1] God seldom announces His affection for someone as publicly as at the baptism of the Son: "You are my Son, whom I love; with you I am well pleased." (Mark 1:11). This declaration heralded the beginning of a grand new phase in Jesus' life. God's proclamation touched the hearts of all those who witnessed this event. God wants to touch our hearts with the same announcement.

"We must learn to accept acceptance," observed Walter Trobisch, a Swiss Christian psychologist.[2] This is one of the great challenges of the spiritual journey—to accept the truth about who we are. It's an integral part of our soul care. This identity gives us purpose, desire, motivation, and the power to endure obstacles, hurt, and challenges along the way. This was true for Jesus, the beloved of God, and it is true for us.

## *Your Soul Identity*

1. How would you describe your identity?
2. What would help you embrace God's view of you?
3. How can you learn to accept self-acceptance?

# 9

# Soul Achievement

God was himself an unwanted child ... an embarrass-
ment to his parents, unexpected, and unplanned. . . .
And still, there has never been a child more wanted,
more loved by God and never a person who became a
greater blessing to more people than Jesus.

INGRID TROBISCH

I have loved you with an everlasting love;
I have drawn you with loving-kindness.

JEREMIAH 31:3

*M*ichael had the ability to be a high achiever in sports. Early in
life his father praised him for his athletic ability. Michael's dad
would cheer and scream for him to make the goal or run for the
touchdown. Yet off the field his father barely spoke to him. He didn't
extend love and acceptance unless Michael performed well. The son
learned that, to gain his father's approval, he had to excel in sports.

Michael's world caved in the day a torn ligament meant no more
sports. After repeated surgeries, he retired from athletics at age six-
teen. He felt the void in his heart grow wider and deeper as he turned
to new interests. Michael felt he would never again be the special
interest of his father.

Expectant parents simply pray that their baby will be healthy.
Once a baby is born strong and well, however, most parents gradually want *more* than just good health. Even average abilities are in-
sufficient. Now what matters is whether that child is the first to walk,
talk, or read. Life becomes a contest to see if the child will make

the team or be the prettiest or the smartest. The unconditional love and acceptance of the nursery very often dissolves into pressure to perform.

As adults, we long to recapture that unconditional love that once was expressed toward us. Instead, we feel the pressure to perform. Personal value is ascribed only for notable achievement. We always need to do more. Our souls risk implosion if we can't accomplish enough. The bar is always too high for one who cannot rest in God's acceptance.

"Just as I am, without one plea"—that's how we come to God.[1] Not as we *think* we should be or *ought* to be, but as we are. God doesn't require a list of accomplishments. He loves us unconditionally, delighting in us. Our worth resides in our identity as the beloved sons and daughters of the Most High God. This is a place of honor. We matter.

### Your Soul Identity

1. Is achievement part of your soul identity? If so, how?
2. What do you want more of in life?
3. Knowing that God loves you, how can you love yourself?

# 10

# The Turning Point

The act of self-acceptance is the root of all things. I must agree to be the person who I am. Agree to have the qualifications which I have. Agree to live with the limitations set for me. . . . The clarity and the courageousness of this acceptance is the foundation of all existence.

ROMANO GUARDINI

Accept one another, then, just as Christ accepted you, in order to bring praise to God.

ROMANS 15:7

At an early age I heard about God's love, but this message never penetrated me until my freshman year at college. Some of my friends seemed to have something I didn't. When I asked them about what was different in their lives, they told me a simple transformational truth—God loved them unconditionally.

This soaked into my heart, and I felt the profound sense of sacred love change me and the direction of my life. This love gave me meaning, a sense of belonging. I discovered purpose when I finally understood that I was the object of God's lavish affection. Many things in my heart, however, did not change instantly. The sticky residue of self-rejection followed me for years.

Like the prodigal son in Jesus' parable, I had looked for love in all the wrong places. But also like the prodigal, I had to "come to my senses," understanding something that had escaped me for a long time (see Luke 15:17). I was loved in the presence of my Father God in a way that I had never been loved before. In God's presence I found the acceptance that I had always dreamed about.

Still, I had to accept God's acceptance, his divine embrace. No other arms could hold me this way. These were not arms folded in rejection. They were extended to offer me my true self and my true home.

Accepting ourselves as the beloved of God is a turning point for Christians, but it can be difficult to accept what Scripture says about self-love. We are told to "love ourselves" (Lev. 19:18; Matt. 22:39; Mark 12:31; Luke 10:27). Paul reminds us that the entire law of God can be summed up in one command: "Love your neighbor as yourself" (Gal. 5:14). He also tells us that "when you add up everything in the law code, the sum total is love" (Rom. 13:10 MSG).

When it comes to God's love, many of us can believe it's true about others but not about ourselves. I can more easily believe that a friend is the beloved of God than to believe it about myself. Yet to love and accept ourselves is a first step in soul care. Without self-love, we compete with others for validation, and we stagnate in jealousy and resentment. We end up battering our souls and the souls of others. Christian psychologist Walter Trobisch reminded us that "without self-love there can be no love for others."[1] Don't we want to give and receive love?

So take the first step. Believe in God's love. Believe it for yourself, for the sake of your soul.

## *Your Soul Identity*

1. Do you love yourself? Do you love your soul?
2. What feelings might surface as you explore loving yourself?
3. What would loving yourself look like?

# 11

# The Divine Embrace

When Jesus looks at us, no matter how we feel about ourselves, he feels delight.

KEN GIRE

He arose and came to his father. But when he was still a great way off, his father saw him and had compassion, and ran and fell on his neck and kissed him.

LUKE 15:20 NKJV

The parable of the prodigal son is one of the most loved stories in the Bible. People can better grasp God's love as they read the dramatic account of the rebellious son who returns home to find a father who's been waiting and waiting for his homecoming. I wonder what it would be like to watch such a reunion. The father runs and passionately embraces his son. It is stunning to imagine.

So many times I've longed to feel God the Father's arms around my neck. But would I be embarrassed? Would I feel small? Would I let myself be loved, even though I was undeserving of such love? Would I allow myself to be embraced by God?

It's hard to imagine this embrace because we know only the touch of other humans. When we fall into the arms of people, there are conditions and limits to the love they offer. An aching heart can fall into any waiting arms, but not all embraces are comforting. We can be grabbed and squeezed by those desperate for love, whose embraces demand and control. We also grab love for ourselves and demand it on our own terms. What we think is love may not be. This love may gratify for the short term, but it never deeply satisfies.

A God who kisses us with affection and embraces us with joy is startling. No doubt most of us struggle with a God who longs to love us lavishly. We can't fathom being loved unconditionally. It makes us uncomfortable. But at the same time, we long for this love to engulf us.

Christian psychologist David Benner puts it this way:

> Regardless of what you have come to believe about God based on your life experience, the truth is that when God thinks of you, love swells in his heart and a smile comes to his face. God bursts with love for humans. He is far from being emotionally uninvolved with his creation. . . . The Christian God chooses to be known as Love, and that love pervades every aspect of God's relationship with us.[1]

If you're still a long way from home, God waits for you. He runs breathlessly toward you. Can you hear him panting? The divine embrace awaits you.

## Your Soul Identity

1. Imagine God loving you unconditionally. How does it feel?
2. How could you actually allow God to lavishly love you?
3. What person comes closest to loving you in such a Godlike way?

# Soul Velcro

There is nothing we can do that will make God love us more. There is nothing we can do that will make God love us less.

PHILIP YANCEY

Discover beauty in everyone.

ROMANS 12:17 MSG

When a preschooler puts on her shoes, she probably doesn't struggle with laces and buckles. Most likely, her shoes fasten together with Velcro, a trademarked product that has changed the way kids—and the rest of us—make shoes "buckle" and other things stick together. The hundreds of uses for this amazing product save time and frustration.

I often wish that someone could create a Soul Velcro. We need spiritual truths to stick to us so that we can live abundantly. Without Velcro in the soul, we don't keep crucial beliefs in place. We can forget that we matter to God. We can ignore what is really true about us and begin to listen to lies whispered into our hearts. We learn, in fact, to doubt that we are loved at all. Lies somehow have a way of sticking to the soul while the answers to these soul rumblings tend not to stick. They slide off our souls without effect.

Ironic, isn't it, that it's the hurtful rather than the healing ideas and comments that "stick" to us? Conventional wisdom claims that criticisms stay with us much longer than do compliments. Perhaps we harbor painful input because it validates what we suspected about ourselves: We're really not who we're hyped to be.

Some of the hurtful lies we hang on to sound like this:

- "You don't have what it takes to be a man."
- "You're not leadership material."
- "You're a bad wife and mother."
- "You're a poser and imposter. You are going to be found out."
- "If you perform well and look good, then you can be loved."

But what if this negativity could just roll off the soul and out of our thoughts?

Imagine God's sacred love filling up and sticking to the soul. If this happened, we would remember God's compassion and not give in to self-contempt and condemnation. We would not hang on to lies. We could accept ourselves as objects of God's passionate affection. We could live securely and not be riddled with anxiety.

Reminding ourselves of God's truth is important. Our identities are derived from believing that God loves us. In other words, allowing God's love to stick to our souls reveals our true identities.

## Your Soul Identity

1. What negative statements have stuck to your soul?
2. What positive truth would you like to stick to your soul?
3. How can you allow God's love and acceptance to stay with you?

# Soulful Indulgence

Faith is trusting fully that God loves me.

HENRI NOUWEN

Long before he laid down earth's foundations, he had us
in mind, had settled on us as the focus of his love, to be
made whole and holy by his love.

EPHESIANS 1:4 MSG

*L*ast week friends invited us out for dinner. We met at their favorite restaurant, and I perked up as the waiter described the special entrées: "Tonight, we have a wonderful, tender Delmonico steak that has marinated for seven days in the rich spices of ginger and teriyaki. It has been rubbed with fresh garlic and cracked black pepper, and then left to indulge itself in the juices of fresh Hawaiian pineapple." I didn't need the menu. My mind was made up. The night would be a feast, with good friends, lingering conversation, and mouthwatering steak.

The description of that steak, its spices and juices, initiated a meaningful conversation that evening. We noted the waiter's choice of two words: *marinate* and *indulge*. While steaks marinate and indulge, people do not.

This is a demanding, grinding world. The efforts of life, work, marriage, children, relationships, and responsibilities often do not allow us to marinate in anything other than worries. If we indulge ourselves, it's to survive. Ours is a 24/7 culture. When we sleep, we get behind. We produce or get replaced. We move forward or we are sidelined. Marinating and indulging are just not words we apply to reality.

I'd like to challenge that reality. We must learn to marinate in God's love. I propose that we indulge ourselves, if for only a few moments each day, as the true objects of God's affection. We are beings who bear the image of God. We are the chosen ones, marked with the intimate passion of a God who chooses to disclose himself to us. In this we should marinate and indulge.

Often in the afternoon my wife, Gwen, has a cup of coffee and a piece of chocolate. She says, "This is my time to indulge myself." This is her time to stop, relax, and enjoy. She savors a few quiet moments with the flavors from a mug of roasted coffee and a single piece of dark chocolate. Perhaps we could apply her habit to our relationship with God, indulging in and enjoying him. It's good for the soul.

## Your Soul Identity

1. How can you adjust your life to indulge in God's love?
2. In what ways can you marinate in this love?
3. How can you awaken your senses to God's love?

# Beloved Others

The greatest gift my friendship can give to you is the gift
of your Belovedness.

HENRI NOUWEN

Behold, you are fair, my love!

Behold, you are fair!

SONG OF SONGS 4:1 NKJV

*A* friend took me out for a drive when I was really down. He
thought the mountain air and scenery would help. It did a little.
But what helped more than anything was when we stopped the car
and headed down a well-worn trail. My friend asked me to sit down.
Then he said, "Steve, I think you've forgotten who you are. I want
to remind you." He told me that I really am the beloved of God. He
said, "No matter how bad you feel inside, Steve, your feelings don't
change who you really are."

Each of us is the beloved of God. Helping others claim and realize
their own belovedness is a privilege and sacred responsibility. This
means we learn to be "for" our friends and family and not against
them. Being for people means that we believe they are God's beloved.

At Jesus' baptism and transfiguration, God speaks of Jesus as the
beloved. For the benefit of both Jesus and those around him, God
said, as paraphrased by Eugene Peterson, "This is my Son, chosen and
marked by my love, delight of my life" (Matt. 3:17 MSG). This statement reminds us of who Jesus is and who we are: the beloved of God.
Think about the people with whom you "do" life. All of these people
need to be reminded of who they really are. We can so easily forget.

When we are told that we are the beloved, we learn to recognize the voice of love that speaks into our hearts. It tells us who we are apart from what we have done or accomplished. This is joy to our hearts because we all long to know our true selves apart from the many masks we wear throughout our lives.

We need to be reminded of who we are because the world and other voices erode our identity and make us feel worthless, insignificant, and unappreciated. Friendship at the soul level is where these words can and should be spoken. When trusted and safe voices speak to us about our belovedness, we learn to accept this as the truth, which it actually is.

We are image bearers of God. In each face, then, is the image of God. Your spouse, child, parent, friend, coworker, pastor, and teacher each reveals to you a certain aspect of the image of God that no other person offers. Each aspect reminds us of the depth and complexity of our heavenly Father, in whose image we are made.

When we speak to each other, reminding one another of our uniqueness and our belovedness, we come to realize that we do offer something no one else offers. This is why reminding and affirming one another of being the beloved is so vitally important.

Community is the place where this should happen. In our competitive workplaces, schools, and world, we won't hear much talk about love. These are places where the language of being the beloved competes with the language of earned acceptance. Our various communities—healthy families; safe friendships; churches—are where we look forward to being accepted, embraced, touched, and recognized for who we are.

## Your Soul Identity

1. Do you believe in the belovedness of others? Why, or why not?
2. How can you affirm the image of God in your friends and family?
3. How can you affirm the image of God in those who seem unlovable?

# PART 3

# SOUL JOURNEY

*Embarking on Your Inner Pathways*

## 15

# Journey of the Soul

I still haven't found what I'm looking for.

U2

Blessed are those whose strength is in you,
who have set their hearts on pilgrimage.

PSALM 84:5

*I*n 1563, the Heidelberg Catechism was composed in Germany to teach young adults essentials of the Christian faith. The first question of this well-known document expresses the root of our soul's journey:

What is your only comfort in life and death?
That I am not my own, but belong—body and soul, in life and death—to my faithful Savior Jesus Christ.

All of us are born with the souls of pilgrims; we search for something better. The answer to the catechism's question describes what our hearts long to find. We are on a journey *to belong.*

High above the floor of the Sistine Chapel in Rome, artist Michelangelo painted a dramatic scene of God creating the world. God's finger points to Adam. Adam's finger stretches toward God. That gap—the distance between the Creator and Adam—is thought by some to represent humanity's journey toward God. Everyone reaches for the divine, but not everyone recognizes the true source of our desires. Consciously or unconsciously, in some way we all try to close the gap.

If we try to fill that gap with people and things, those can never occupy a place that only God can fill. No amount of money, no benchmark of success, no mortal can close this gap. That's because our life journeys are spiritual, beyond the acquisitions of this world. Augustine of Hippo, an early church father, said, "You have made us for yourself, and our heart is restless until it rests in you."[1] These are journey words, expressing the true longing of our souls.

Augustine's fourth-century prayer still describes restless pilgrims today. We long to fill the gap between God's sacred fingertip and our trembling hand. Our journey will converge with the way, truth, and life of Jesus Christ. His way fills the gap. His truth becomes our truth. His life touches ours. Jesus becomes the "what" we've been looking for all along.

### Your Soul Journey

1. What are you looking for?
2. How have you tried to close the gap between God and you?
3. What does it mean to belong to God?

# 16

# Checking the Dipstick

Does your spiritual life sometimes seem more like a burden than a blessing? Does your spirituality seem to exhaust you as often as it refreshes you? Have your spiritual practices become "just another thing to do" in an already overcrowded, stress-filled schedule? If so, then you need to simplify your spiritual life.

DONALD S. WHITNEY

Let's take a good look at the way we're living
and reorder our lives under GOD.

LAMENTATIONS 3:40 MSG

When you check the oil in a car, you lift the hood, find the dipstick, pull it out, and determine whether enough oil is in the engine to lubricate the parts. A car needs oil to run properly. If no oil is flowing through the gears of the engine, friction will ruin the inner mechanism.

I learned this lesson the hard way several years ago. Our family had planned a camping trip in the mountains of North Carolina. Fall lingered in the air. The oak leaves were turning orange, yellow, and red. It was the perfect weekend to go camping. The six of us piled into our van. We pulled a camper trailer for a getaway weekend. I had looked forward to this trip for months. We'd marked it on our calendars and had not accepted invitations to do anything else. When Friday arrived, we started the adventure and drove an hour and a half to reach the state park. We started early so we'd have the best possible campsite.

About five miles from the camping area, the van's engine died.

Without warning, we stopped dead in our tracks. We sat in what seemed the middle of nowhere, stranded. I managed to flag down a passing motorist who took me to a house where I called for help. About two hours later, as dark descended, an old tow truck pulled up behind us. The driver checked the van's engine and said, "Mister, this engine is blown." The engine was "blown" because there was no oil in it.

After that, the blown engine became an important symbol in our lives. In the midst of busyness and ministry, I had not maintained my van. It was now too late to simply get a read on the engine by checking the dipstick. It was an expensive mistake. The van needed a replacement engine. That weekend, as the van's engine was replaced, I looked at my own internal engine. The state of my soul was crying out for some serious maintenance.

The soul functions much like a car's engine. If we want to function properly for life's long haul, we need to check our soul's dipstick. Imagine a dipstick being lowered into the core of your soul, then pulled out for inspection. What does it indicate? What does it smell like? The answer might be . . .

- "I'm about two quarts low."
- "It looks pretty crude. I need help."
- "I don't even have a reading on the stick. There must be no oil at all."

If you practice this exercise and get a low reading on your soul's dipstick, it's time for attention. To avoid burnout, exhaustion, and fatigue, start maintaining your soul now.

### Your Soul Journey

1. If you could read your internal engine with a dipstick, what would it tell you about your soul? Describe the level indicator, the smell, and the oil's quality.
2. If your soul is about to run on empty, how can you rescue it from burnout?
3. How can you periodically check the condition of your soul?

# 17

# Embracing the Present

God cannot give us a happiness and peace apart from himself, because it is not there. There is no such thing.

C. S. LEWIS

I have learned the secret of being content in any and every situation, whether well fed or hungry, whether living in plenty or in want.

PHILIPPIANS 4:12

*I* know a couple who seemed to live for retirement. Both worked hard in their careers, lived frugally and saved. They planned to travel frequently, visiting exciting places they had only read and dreamed about.

One week prior to retirement, they bought a new motorized recreation vehicle. They attended retirement parties and packed. But they never set out on that first trip. Instead, the husband learned from a doctor that he had terminal cancer. Within a few months his widow sat bewildered, confused, and angry. "Why did we wait so long to start living?" she asked.

This couple put their lives "on hold" for the future. They never learned to embrace the present. Embracing the present means to live now, not waiting. Embracing the present means choosing to live without regrets. It means making conscientious choices to live the life you desire now, not later.

On a recent trip, a friend and I browsed through a bookstore and noticed the books written to help us gain the life we want . . . later. At my friend's encouragement, I bought a book about planning for retirement. We'd just had a troubling conversation about whether Gwen and I would have enough in the bank to retire. He motivated me or perhaps scared me to think about my future in more detail. I read the book on the flight home.

The book advised saving to enjoy life later by avoiding purchases now. It got down to incidentals, like buying a caffe latte. The author told me that if I saved my three dollars now rather than buying my coffee, in twenty years I'd have a phenomenal sum of cash with which to buy my own Starbucks franchise.

But seriously, what if I want to sit on a bench, sipping my latte *now*, enjoying time in the park as I watch people walk by? What if coffee is my link to spending time with my wife or friends? It is important to save, but it also is important to live in the present.

Jesus said, "I came so they can have real and eternal life, more and better life than they ever dreamed of" (John 10:10 MSG). Is this "more and better life" only reserved for heaven? Jesus' teaching on life in his kingdom is both in the future and in the "here and now."

Soul care means living in the present.

### Your Soul Journey

1. How can you say "yes" to each day?
2. How can you be fulfilled in the present?
3. How do you define contentment?

## 18

# Accepting the Past

Leave the irreparable past in his hands, and step out into
the irresistible future with him.

OSWALD CHAMBERS

Review the past for me,
    let us argue the matter together;
    state the case for your innocence.

ISAIAH 43:26

*I* was in a hurry to catch my plane. I threw some stuff in my suitcase—clothes, books, and materials for the conference. At the airline check-in counter, I placed my bag on the scale. My heart sank as I saw that my bag was well over the weight limit. The airline agent politely said, "Sir, you need to get rid of some things in this bag, or it's going to be very expensive for you."

When the airline agent moved to the next person, I tried to smile, but inside I panicked. I took stuff from the bag and jammed it into my carry-on. At that moment, it seemed I needed everything I'd packed. I couldn't leave any stuff behind.

Traveling through life with heavy emotional baggage also is costly. The stuff of past unresolved issues, wounds, and broken relationships can weigh us down and steal joy and hope. We hope that past sin and pain can somehow be stuffed away or rearranged in our baggage. Soul care means that we need to make peace with the past. Making peace means "working through" until we accept what happened. We don't try to cut it off as if it doesn't matter.

On our wedding day, my wife married a man with a heritage of family quirks, customs that were different from her own, issues that she wasn't expecting, and personal habits that previously had been hidden. Accepting my past has taken both of us time, effort, and grace. I am, after all, a project still in process. I'm still becoming who God wants me to be. I need grace and forgiveness. When I accept my past, I admit who I am. I acknowledge my desire to change and recognize that I will still fail.

The future irresistibly propels us forward, not back. Once when I was at my wits end in my work, I felt guilty and ashamed about mistakes. I wanted to quit. I was frustrated and overwhelmed at the thought of how little progress I'd made. A dear friend listened to my lament about all that had gone wrong. After I stopped talking, my friend said, "Steve, keep coming forward." Those words, spoken without judgment and blame, offered grace and acceptance. They simply encouraged me to take the next step.

The apostle Paul offered wise advice about the past. He said, "But one thing I do: Forgetting what is behind and straining toward what is ahead, I press on" (Phil. 3:13b–14a). Our confidence grows in taking steps forward. Accepting the past unleashes the grace to begin again.

## Your Soul Journey

1. What troubles you about your past? Have you made peace with it?
2. How has God redeemed your past?
3. As you accept the past, what do you need to do differently?

# Relinquishing the Future

The best thing about the future is that it comes only one day at a time.

ABRAHAM LINCOLN

What I'm trying to do here is to get you to relax, to not be so preoccupied with getting, so you can respond to God's giving. People who don't know God and the way he works fuss over these things, but you know both God and how he works. Steep your life in God-reality, God-initiative, God-provisions. Don't worry about missing out.

MATTHEW 6:31–33 MSG

My oldest son is a soldier in the U.S. Army. As this is written, he will be deployed in just a few weeks to fight in a war. Just writing these words conjures up all sorts of thoughts, and ties my soul in a knot. As he goes into "harm's way," I find myself in a season of deep questions and anxiety. All of this stirs a challenge: How can I release my son to the future when so much seems to be at stake? I know the Bible tells me not to be anxious. But when I think of my son's future, I feel the fear deep inside.

Soul care means learning to relax in the present without trying to control the future. In Matthew 6:34, Jesus tells us, "Therefore do not worry about tomorrow, for tomorrow will worry about itself. Each day has enough trouble of its own."

Fear of the unknown can wreak havoc in our souls. For me, worry seems to come easy in the night. When it's dark and my wife is asleep, I can imagine all the possible things that might go wrong. The "what ifs" keep my head spinning and cause my soul grief. At the core of all this worry is the belief that life is up to me, and if something is going to happen, I need to make it happen myself, without anyone's assistance. This is a subtle form of idolatry. I leave God out of the picture and imagine myself as having all the control. Nothing could be further from the truth.

In Eugene Peterson's paraphrase of Matthew 6:33–34 (MSG), Jesus says,

> Steep your life in God-reality, God-initiative, God-provisions. Don't worry about missing out. You'll find all your everyday human concerns will be met.
>
> Give your entire attention to what God is doing right now, and don't get worked up about what may or may not happen tomorrow. God will help you deal with whatever hard things come up when the time comes.

When we try to implement these words, it doesn't take long to realize our anxieties about the future. Nagging questions taunt us. Will I meet the right person? Will I get the job offer? Is my loved one going to be safe?

Much of the Christian life is about "letting go." When we adopt the heart attitude that Jesus recommended, we relinquish the future, and trust God with the outcome. We learn in "letting go" to trust God in a whole new way. Relinquishment then becomes a reality, not a theoretical concept. We believe that God keeps our best interests in his heart.

Ultimately, circumstances force us to answer two questions time and again: Is God good? Can God do what he has said he will do? How we respond to these questions determines the condition of our souls. When we relinquish control of the future, we relax in God's goodness and his ability to be himself, show himself to us, and give himself to us. Believing that God is good helps us to embrace God as a loving Father whose goodness reaches us no matter what. We say with Paul, "That's why we can be so sure that every detail in our lives of love for God is worked into something good" (Rom. 8:28 MSG). To relinquish helps us accept the goodness of God. We learn to relax in the hands of God, whose character is good. We wrestle with events and developments in our lives, but ultimately we are brought back to whether we believe that God is good, no matter what.

The psalmist David reduces the complexity of God's character and actions to two fundamental aspects of his heart: "You, O God, are strong, and . . . you, O Lord, are loving" (Ps. 62:11–12). I believe this verse might be one of the most important and insightful verses about God. Knowing that God is strong and believing that God is loving helps us relinquish control and relax, trusting his hands to give us what we truly need in life.

Do you believe that God is both strong and loving? How you answer that question will help shape your soul's ability to relinquish the future.

### *Your Soul Journey*

1. Do you believe that God is good? Why, or why not?
2. Do you think God will do what he has promised? Why, or why not?
3. How can you begin to relinquish control of your future?

# 20

# The Story of Exodus

The most comprehensive term for what God is doing to
get us out of the mess we are in is salvation. Salvation is
God doing for us what we can't do for ourselves.

EUGENE PETERSON

God himself is at rest. And at the end of the journey we'll
surely rest with God.

HEBREWS 4:10 MSG

The Exodus is lived out in the story of every person. Oxford theologian Alister McGrath writes,

> Each of us has a personal journey to make, from our own
> Egypt to our promised land. We have left something behind
> in order to make this journey. We have had to break free
> from our former lives in order to begin afresh. *We* were in
> Egypt. *We* were delivered from bondage. *We* are in the wilderness, on our way to the promised land. The story of the
> Exodus involves us—because it is *about* us.[1]

The Israelites were held hostage in a foreign land and oppressed
for years in horrible conditions. In exchange for slave labor, they
lived for generations with only the hope of another life. God raised
up Moses, who reluctantly accepted the task of leading them into
liberation and freedom. Once they were miraculously set free, they
entered a long period in the wilderness. After the wilderness experience, they finally entered the place that God had promised them—
the Promised Land.

There are four distinct stages to the Exodus: (1) bondage; (2) liberation; (3) wilderness; and (4) promised land. Each Christian is in one of these movements.

Even Christians can be in *bondage* to many different things. Something in our past could make us feel enslaved. We're surviving but not living, knowing deep inside that we're in a place where we don't belong. We wait helplessly to be set free and wonder when freedom will arrive.

*Liberation* sets us free. We dream of freedom in work, freedom in relationships; freedom to be our true selves; freedom from our past; freedom from mistakes, guilt, and sin. Liberation happens when an alcoholic admits his attachment to the bottle, puts it down, and intentionally walks away. It is realizing that what God wants for me and what I want may not be too far apart. Liberation happens when you finally decide that what you really want and desire may not be bad after all, and you do it. It feels freeing to do this one thing. It could involve a job, a difficult choice, or the decision to live out a dream.

We walk into *wilderness* when we lose our way, don't know where we are, or lack direction to where we want to be. A wilderness experience is a season of being on our own and lacking direction. The wilderness often comes unannounced and uninvited. Grief, for example, and the journey through losing someone or something is a wilderness. Wilderness is an aimless existence, having the sense of drifting. It's when God seems silent and distant, and you question whether he cares about or even knows your predicament.

The *promised land* is where you arrive and recognize the place you've been traveling toward as your true home. It's heaven in the long run, the place where all that God is becomes visible and real, and where we live in security, free from threat. But other promised lands reveal themselves in the short run—when we find a respite from the journey in a person, a place, a book, or an experience, a place of convergence. In this place of spiritual shelter, questions get answered and the dots get connected. The promised land can also be a time when hope is restored and when promise is fulfilled.

The Exodus story offers us a language to tell the story of our souls. The stages of the Exodus present us with options and choices, and allow us a place to work through our reactions and responses. The Exodus is a true story that helps us understand our own journeys of the soul.

### Your Soul Journey

1. Where are you in the Exodus story—Bondage? Liberation? Wilderness? Moving into the Promised Land?
2. How can you tend to your soul during this time?
3. What would your promised land look like?

## 21

# The Process of Endurance

Remember that you have only one soul; that you have
only one death to die; that you have only one life.... If
you do this, there will be many things about which you
care nothing.

TERESA OF AVILA

For you have need of endurance.

HEBREWS 10:36 NKJV

Several years ago I watched the women's summer Olympics marathon on television. A Scandinavian woman was trying to finish
the race. The other competitors had completed the race, and cameras
captured her grueling struggle to finish. She wobbled and zigzagged
toward the finish line. The crowds ecstatically cheered her on. Every
step looked like sheer agony, but she endured and crossed the finish
line, a victor of sorts.

The Greek word that can be translated "endure" means "to remain under." To endure something, then, is to remain under its influence. An athlete endures practice and rigorous training in order
to perform at his or her best. Without "remaining under" training
and discipline, there is no winning.

I often watched my son's high school football team practices. After a long day of practice, some of the players would be ready to quit.
The coach would scream out, "No guts, no glory!" He inspired them
on to victory and the glory that awaited them. The challenge to endure the hard work paid off, and that year the team reached the state
playoffs.

Hebrews 11–12 speaks about endurance, especially as we follow the examples of the pioneers of our faith. They endured years in the wilderness, unfair treatment, failure, disbelief, imprisonment, rejection, and death. Many challenges they faced are difficult to comprehend. Through their lives we catch a glimpse of transforming truths for ourselves.

Suffering was inescapable for these ancient pilgrims. By enduring, they learned valuable lessons that they couldn't learn when life was going smoothly. Through the enduring seasons, they testified to God's faithfulness, to God's purpose in hard times, to the cost of faith, and to the journey of the faithful. They remained under hard times and showed us how to get through similar difficulties. When we "remain under," we learn truths, lessons, insights, and perspectives that seem priceless.

Enduring difficulty and struggle can be painful. That Olympic athlete running an exhausting marathon looked awkward. Her flailing arms were not graceful. Her stride was inconsistent. Her form at the finish was not what it was at the start. Those years of wilderness trekking were awkward for Moses. Mary's pregnancy, shrouded in mystery and subjected to ridicule, must have felt awkward. Paul's near-death experiences in his travels left him clinging to life, but he became a different man.

The soul, too, needs to endure. The spiritual life is not easy. The journey calls for a steady faith and a heart to persevere, even though we're flailing about. During these times, we can take comfort in Paul's prayer of endurance: "We pray that you'll have the strength to stick it out over the long haul—not the grim strength of gritting your teeth but the glory-strength God gives. It is strength that endures the unendurable and spills over into joy, thanking the Father who makes us strong enough to take part in everything bright and beautiful that he has for us" (Col. 1:11–12 MSG).

*Your Soul Journey*

1. What are you "remaining under" now?
2. Why is "remaining under" a difficult challenge?
3. How can you experience the reality of Paul's prayer? How will you experience "glory-strength"?

# PART 4

# SOUL FORMATION

*Discovering the Influences*
*That Shape You*

## 22

# The Formative Years

Your life is not a problem to be solved but a gift to be opened.

WAYNE MULLER

Being confident of this, that he who began a good work in you will carry it on to completion until the day of Christ Jesus.

PHILIPPIANS 1:6

*I* read through the Sunday morning bulletin of the church I was visiting to get a grasp of how people were informed of ministry opportunities. I also glanced at a list of adult education classes available for visitors. There were classes for different age groups. What struck me was the name of the class for older adults: "Formative Souls."

The *formative* designation usually is applied to stages of child development through early adolescence. During these years, awareness of surroundings, love, and family shape the soul. All who study human development agree that the early years are of great importance.

Yet, this older adults group bravely advertised that they were still in their formative years. In fact, we all are, so long as we live. Throughout our lives, God works the clay. No matter what our stage, God can still use circumstances and events to bring about deep change, according to his plan.

I watched my mother-in-law's soul be shaped in excruciating ways as she awaited her imminent death. She had terminal cancer, and the end of her life was near. During her final few weeks, I watched her soul being readied for death. She asked us to read specific verses from the Bible. She wanted us to sing hymns about heaven and eternal life. She asked for each child and grandchild to come to her bedside for a final private time. She was simply blessing each person in her family with powerful words of love, affirmation, and appreciation. It was a beautiful time to witness. While it was heart-wrenching to watch her slip from us, I was stunned at how incredibly important those bedside times were for her and her family. It was a time of being formed and molded to understand the beauty and significance of dying well.

Each of us is shaped by experiences and people. All along the journey of life God uses sickness and health, defeat and victory, and hard times and good to shape the souls of those he loves.

Lyle Dorsett reminds us,

> This transformation into Christ likeness, holiness, or Christian maturity—whatever rhetoric one chooses to use—is realized in different ways by each person. But the rapidity and depth of the process is directly related to a person's willingness to cooperate with the Holy Spirit's guidance, and most certainly spiritual growth is nurtured or hindered by the quality of teaching and mentoring one finds.[1]

Every day is an opportunity to be formed and shaped more. We are never really "done" with being shaped this side of heaven. There's much to learn; experiences to share and insights to gain in each step and season of life.

## Your Soul Shaping

1. What defining moments has God used to shape your soul in deep ways?
2. How can we more easily cooperate with God in the process of our soul shaping rather than resist him?
3. What particular people has God placed in your life to help shape you now? How have these people helped shaped you in positive ways?

# 23

# Messy Work

My life is a mess.... For as long as I can remember, I
have wanted to be a godly person. Yet when I look at the
yesterdays of my life, what I see, mostly, is a broken, ir-
regular path littered with mistakes and failure. I have had
temporary successes and isolated moments of closeness
to God, but I long for the continuing presence of Jesus.

MICHAEL YACONELLI

What I'm getting at, friends, is that you should simply
keep on doing what you've done from the beginning. . . .
Better yet, redouble your efforts. Be energetic in your life
of salvation, reverent and sensitive before God.

PHILIPPIANS 2:12 MSG

*B*eing a Christian isn't for those who don't want to get soiled. It's
messy work to embark on a path toward spiritual transformation.
Riddled by feelings of what we "ought" to be and do, we can find
ourselves bogged down in a quagmire of guilt, shame, and spiritual
oppression. Deep inside, we recognize the mess we're in, but we hope
no one will find out.

Spiritual and personal change is not a clean, clear-cut process.
Like clay whirled on a potter's wheel. God seems to offer repeated
opportunities to change. We start, stop, start over, go back, redo, and
never quite feel complete.

We get fired. We are diagnosed with cancer. We learn that our
teenage daughter is pregnant or has a drug problem. Then we experience the messiness of life and faith. The same is true when we

ourselves fall into addiction, wrestle with relationships, or drown in doubt. When principles, programs, and how-to steps fail, we can let ourselves be embraced by the Potter's hands. Remarkably, he seems to love a marred, broken pot.

No earthly potter works with clean hands from the moment of first taking hold of the mess to work out impurities in the clay. Likewise, the hands of God are intimately involved in the messy yet glorious process of changing us. His hands touch, press, caress, assure, squash, and stroke. He hovers over our transformation. The work of the Potter's hands is a visible extension of his heart, love, and goodness. Could it be that the Potter loves messes?

The divine Potter makes masterpieces out of messes. We bring the mess. The Potter works the transformation.

## Your Soul Shaping

1. How would you describe your mess right now?
2. How can you see God working in the mess?
3. What outcome do you hope for?

# 24

# The Wake of Formation

Whenever two people meet there are really six people present. There is each man as he sees himself, each as the other person sees him, and each man as he really is.

WILLIAM JAMES

> Deep calls to deep
> in the roar of your waterfalls;
> all your waves and breakers
> have swept over me.

PSALM 42:7

*I* grew up near a lake in North Carolina. Skiing, boating, and swimming were part of my childhood. I remember skiing and jumping the wake of the boat that my father drove. I enjoyed jumping the wakes and the thrill of air underneath my skis as we sped across placid coves. I'd feverishly point to huge cabin cruisers moving down the lake. While on skis, I'd point toward the bigger boats so he'd take me close enough to jump their wakes. The bigger the wake, the greater the thrill.

People also leave wakes behind. The sheer force, volume, and intensity of certain people's wakes can feel like an emotional tsunami. They rock our world. If we don't know how to navigate the wakes of powerful or destructive people, we can be dashed and nearly drowned.

Bill leaves a huge wake. He's had five management jobs in various organizations. In each work situation, conflict emerged as his team felt washed over and marginalized. His power demeaned people until they felt insignificant. He left a trail of washed-up relationships until he finally was fired. Bill didn't understand the problem until he finally was made to face the truth. Over time, he's making changes.

Understanding your soul's wake is an important part of knowing and loving yourself. It is examining your unique design, offering yourself to God so that he can soften the rough edges that hurt other people and cause havoc. Exploring your wake brings insight to the force you bring to relationships, teams, and community. Examining your wake in a safe community helps build a healthy community and families.

Wakes can leave a powerful and positive impression. The wake of a school teacher can be a life-defining encounter for a student. Our youngest son had a teacher like that in the eighth grade. This teacher lifted our son to renewed commitment and enjoyment of classroom learning. Somehow, she inspired him to want to study. Something connected inside his soul that had been missing.

Think about Jesus Christ. He moved with strength and tenderness, truth and grace, and he created ripples that have become an eternal wake. Oh, to become like him.

### Your Soul Shaping

1. To learn about your own wake, ask three people you know to be candid in answering the questions, What is it like to live with me? To work with me? To be with me?
2. Imagine the wake of Jesus. How would you describe life in his wake?
3. Has your wake hurt anyone? Do you need to ask for forgiveness?

# 25

# The Misshapen Soul

Children value themselves to the degree that they have
been valued.

DOROTHY CORKILLE BRIGGS

Take a good look at my trouble, and help me—
I haven't forgotten your revelation.
Take my side and get me out of this;
give me back my life, just as you promised.

PSALM 119:153–154 MSG

*J*oe was thirty-five and attending graduate school. While playing soccer he was hit hard and knocked unconscious by another
player. His friends took him to the hospital, where a series of tests
and x-rays led the doctor to ask, "What happened to you? Your ribs
look like a battlefield." The doctor's words caught Joe off guard. But
the x-rays revealed that every rib had been broken and some multiple
times. This revelation led Joe back to his parents, where he learned
about his internal injuries. Joe had known for a long time that something felt "broken inside." Now he knew the whole story. For the first
time in his life, my friend discovered that both his body and soul had
been battered by parents who had physically and emotionally abused
him. As a result, Joe's soul was badly misshapen.

*Abuse* is a word that brings up painful memories for many people.
When people suffer from abuse, more is assaulted than their bodies. Their souls also suffer. Sexual, emotional, spiritual, and physical
abuses leave hemorrhaging emotional wounds and deep psychic scars.
Consequently, victims of abuse lug around misshapen souls. Whether

abuse happens by intent or neglect, these souls do not receive what they need to thrive. A gaping inner wound seems to defy cure.

Many victims of abuse feel as if their souls are so bruised, they will never fully live. Support groups, prayer, retreats, counseling, and friendship help, but the private pain of someone who has suffered at the hands of another misshapen soul leaves what feels like an unhealable wound. Abused people are left asking, "Why did this happen to me?" "Where was God when this happened?" "Why didn't God protect me?" These questions need to be explored with safe people. Wounded souls need love and grace from healers, but also from family, friends, and church members. They need the healing presence of a community that reflects Christ's compassion.

When we confront abuse and inch toward healing, we can remember the life of Jesus Christ. Jesus did not escape the wounds of mistreatment. He was a "man of sorrows" (Isa. 53:3), hated and rejected; his life filled with sorrow and suffering. When we reflect on the abuse Christ experienced, we can draw into a deeper intimacy with him and know "the fellowship of His sufferings" (Phil. 3:10 NKJV). Through our own sufferings, we can better identify with his. In turn, we can ask him to reshape our souls. Better than anyone, he understands wounds, scars, and healing.

## *Your Soul Shaping*

1. Describe someone you know who has a misshapen soul.
2. What is the best way to love someone who has a misshapen soul?
3. How do our wounds draw us closer to Christ?

# 26

# Shaped by the Psalms

The Psalms in Hebrew are earthy and rough. They are not
genteel. They are not the prayers of nice people couched
in cultural language.

EUGENE PETERSON

The law of the LORD is perfect,
reviving the soul.
The statutes of the LORD are trustworthy,
making wise the simple.

PSALM 19:7

Ancient Jews and early Christians used the psalms as their songs
in worship, though Christians quickly added hymns about Jesus'
life, death, and resurrection. Psalms were set to music and sung. By
singing and reading the ancient poems written by David and other
authors, worshipers have articulated the deepest feelings of the
soul.

The psalms express such clear and universal feelings that they
are used for worship, weddings, funerals, and personal devotions.
About half of them are reactions to trouble in the psalmist's life. We
don't have to know all of the reasons the author was in distress to
hear the cries for help. The psalmist's honesty helps us articulate the
deep stirring of our own souls. Other psalms express joy, praise, and
gratitude for God's goodness and deliverance.

The psalms are a mirror of the soul; in them we see ourselves.
Such honest words speak comfort, lead us in the way, and express
our craving for soul care.

- Psalms state our need to be revived and restored (see Pss. 23; 62; 119:25).
- Psalms articulate spiritual hunger and thirst for what only God provides (Pss. 42; 63).
- Psalms explore the awe and wonder of God's creation (see Pss. 19; 139).
- Psalms model courageous and honest dialogue with God, describing disappointment, despair, and feelings of abandonment (see Pss. 10; 42).
- Psalms express a need for intimacy with God, to be at peace and satisfied in Him (see Pss. 84; 131).
- Psalms look at the wonder of God's Word (see Pss. 19; 119).
- Psalms explore the worship of God (see Pss. 100; 103).

The psalms can shape our souls. They say what words do not easily express—about our God, our relationships, and ourselves. In doing so, they work like finely crafted tools, exposing the soul, revealing the best and worst in us.

Ancient Hebrews listened to the psalms for comfort and guidance. As a Jew, Jesus read from the Psalms, and Christians have followed his example for two millennia. In letting that devotion leave its imprint on us, we can also be shaped.

## Your Soul Shaping

1. Choose one of the psalms mentioned above. What insights do you gain from the psalmist's own soul? How do the psalmist's words help you?
2. How could the psalms specifically contribute to your soul care?
3. Do you have a favorite psalm? How could a favorite psalm shape you?

# 27

# Grow Your Soul

Even if I knew that tomorrow the world would go to
pieces, I would still plant my apple tree.

MARTIN LUTHER KING JR.

A God-shaped life is a flourishing tree.

PROVERBS 11:28 MSG

*F*riends from our church asked us to attend the dedication to God
of their newborn son. The couple asked the invited guests to take
turns using a shovel to dig a hole for a young tree to be planted in the
child's honor. As we dug, we acknowledged how each person would
have a role in the spiritual growth of this child. As we gathered to
pray, we dedicated both the tree and the child to God's hands. In our
prayer we voiced the needs for growth, protection, and vitality in
this life that was beginning.

Soul care resembles a tree. It takes years for a tender tree to ma-
ture. Time, attention, nourishment, protection, and pruning contribute to its growth. The same is true for spiritual growth. While
some people grow and change quickly and dramatically, most of us
grow gradually and quietly, like a tree.

Eugene Peterson calls the Christian journey "a long obedience in
the same direction."[1] Our inner growth can be long and arduous. At
other times, it's joyful and spontaneous. Different seasons usher in
different challenges. A summer drought can wither a tree's health.
The fall initiates loss. A cold winter can break brittle limbs. Spring
brings new surges of growth. During any season, the proper care
shields a tree—and us—from irreparable damage.

The feeding of our spiritual roots provides the nourishment for a vibrant and resilient soul. We take in the nourishment of God's Word to grow into maturity (1 Peter 2:2). Just as the apple tree grows to produce its fruit—apples—we grow to produce fruit of the Spirit—the character of Jesus Christ. Still, there are no shortcuts to cultivating our souls. It is a day-by-day, year-to-year process that does not respond to a set formula for success. But the long process enables the development of an intimate relationship with God.

The Creator provides the sun and rain to nurture a tree's growth. We can trust him to also provide what we need to grow the soul.

## Your Soul Shaping

1. What do you need to grow spiritually?
2. What could nourish your spiritual life? Why?
3. Using the metaphor of a tree, at what stage of growth are you?

## 28

# Soul Hospitality

Never give a hollow greeting of peace or turn away someone who needs your love.

BENEDICT OF NURSIA

He gave him first aid, disinfecting and bandaging his
wounds. Then he lifted him onto his donkey, led him to
an inn, and made him comfortable. In the morning he
took out two silver coins and gave them to the innkeeper,
saying, "Take good care of him. If it costs any more, put
it on my bill—I'll pay you on my way back."

LUKE 10:34–35 MSG

Jesus' parable of the Good Samaritan in Luke 10:25–37 was radical. It begins with a man being beaten and left half dead. He desperately needs help and mercy. Religious people pass by the needy
man, not once but twice. Finally a traditional enemy of Jews, a Samaritan, goes out of his way to provide care and safety.

Jesus used the story to reveal a deeper truth about soul care. The
people who his listeners thought would help did not. They passed by
the man, looking the other way. It was the man with every reason to
pass by who took the victim to an inn for nourishment and reviving.
He had compassion, so he did not pass by.

Many people know the feeling of being passed. Alone, without
friends or community ties, they feel forgotten and without value.
They need the attention that will heal their souls. Even the simplest
acts of hospitality, offered at a point of need by unexpected pilgrims,
can touch people deep within.

Hospitality means the gracious treatment of guests. The Bible tells us to practice it regularly and wholeheartedly. Consider these instructions and examples:

- "When a foreigner lives with you in your land, don't take advantage of him. Treat the foreigner the same as a native. Love him like one of your own. Remember that you were once foreigners in Egypt. I am GOD, your God" (Lev. 19:33–34 MSG).
- "There was an estate nearby that belonged to Publius, the chief official of the island. He welcomed us to his home and for three days entertained us hospitably" (Acts 28:7).
- "Help needy Christians; be inventive in hospitality" (Rom. 12:13 MSG).
- "Offer hospitality to one another without grumbling" (1 Peter 4:9).
- "Keep on loving each other as brothers. Do not forget to entertain strangers, for by so doing some people have entertained angels without knowing it" (Heb. 13:1–2).
- "So they deserve any support we can give them. In providing meals and a bed, we become their companions in spreading the Truth" (3 John 8 MSG).

Sometimes the place of hospitality matters more than anything else we can do. In Christ's parable, the injured man wasn't offered a program or a book. He was taken to the place of sanctuary. It was a place of transformation back to health. Here, life flowed back into a badly beaten body and soul, aided by the healing hands of time. Likewise, love requires that soul injured travelers be taken to a hospital for the soul, a necessary respite for a weary soul. In this special place, the victim heals.

We all need the solace of an inn to reshape our souls, a place to talk, have oil applied to wounds, and rest. Where is your place? When you're revived, what place can you offer to others?

## Your Soul Shaping

1. Do you have an inn-like place to which you can retreat?
2. What ingredients do you need for a time of healing, spiritual renewal, or rest?
3. How does Jesus serve us as the Innkeeper for souls?

# PART 5

# SOUL EXERCISES

*Practicing the Spiritual Disciplines*

29

# The Need to Practice

The spiritual life is first of all a life. It is not merely something to be known and studied, it is to be lived.

THOMAS MERTON

Physical exercise has some value, but spiritual exercise is much more important, for it promises a reward in both this life and the next.

1 TIMOTHY 4:8 NLT

*P*hysical conditioning is a multi-billion-dollar-a-year business. Gyms and fitness centers provide the places, tools, and inspiration to get into shape. But how do we take care of our souls? Throughout the church's history, spiritual exercises have proved effective for soul care. You might know these as spiritual disciplines or holy habits. They make room for God in our lives.

Physical exercise promotes health for the body. Soul exercises promote healthy relationship with God and others. Soul exercises train us to be spiritually alive and resilient. Practicing these strengthens the soul.

Soul exercises connect us to God. Think of soul exercises like physical exercises. Sit-ups improve the stomach muscles. Push-ups improve our arm muscles. Different exercises develop different parts of the body. Likewise, soul exercises work on different parts of our spiritual life and our relationships.

We learn about soul exercises by reading how Jesus practiced his faith and modeled for us how to do life. Note the following in regard to soul exercises.

- Jesus practiced prayer (Mark 1:35; Luke 6:12).
- Jesus practiced fasting (Matt. 4:2).
- Jesus practiced silence and solitude (Luke 5:16; 21:37).
- Jesus practiced celebration (John 2:1–11; 12:1–8).

As we observe Jesus engaging in exercises for his soul and see the resulting benefits, we are motivated to follow his example. Consider these verses, paraphrased from Scripture in *The Message*.

- "Watch what God does, and then you do it" (Eph. 5:1).
- "Anyone who claims to be intimate with God ought to live the same kind of life Jesus lived" (1 John 2:6).
- "This is the kind of life you've been invited into, the kind of life Christ lived. He suffered everything that came his way so you would know that it could be done, and also know how to do it, step-by-step" (1 Peter 2:21).

As modeled by Christians for two thousand years, soul exercises can include study, worship, prayer, service, fellowship, confession, celebration, journaling, solitude, silence, fasting, secrecy, sacrifice, meditation, and more.[1] We can choose to do what fits our needs and personalities. As we grow spiritually, we can vary exercises. However we practice, the goal is to draw closer to God. The exercises are the means by which a child converses with and learns more about the heavenly Father. Such times are to be desired, not practiced legalistically, by coercion, or because of guilt.

The Christian life concerns more than amassing knowledge about God. We want to experience God. Jesus practiced soul exercises and maintained spiritual disciplines. If the Son of God did this, why shouldn't we?

## *Your Soul Exercises*

1. Do you practice soul exercises? If so, which do you enjoy?
2. In what areas would you like to further strengthen your spiritual life? What would help you grow in those ways?
3. What soul exercise could contribute to growth?

## 30

# Cries of the Soul

Prayer is the soul's sincere desire, unuttered or expressed,
the motion of a hidden fire that trembles in the breast.

JAMES MONTGOMERY

During the days of Jesus' life on earth, he offered up
prayers and petitions with loud cries and tears to the one
who could save him from death, and he was heard because of his reverent submission.

HEBREWS 5:7–8

*I*n recent years, my wife and I have found ourselves in desperate
and trying times. My wife's mother died. My wife became a cancer survivor. (Even as I type that word *survivor,* am I really sure she
is?) Our youngest son nearly died of complications from a ruptured
appendix. I lost my job. We encountered medical insurance night-
mares. The future looked frightening.

We were broken, humbled, and left searching for answers. We had
many questions and requests. Some of the answers came slowly. Often we felt empty of meaningful words to say. All of this made me
want to see how Jesus handled the hard times in his life. What could
I learn by looking at his example?

Hebrews 5:7 offered encouragement to me by showing how to
pray when life is hard. Jesus "offered up prayers and petitions with
loud cries and tears to the one who could save him. . . ." Loud cries?
Tears? Jesus' prayers were intense. They must have been filled with
emotion. Deep passion emerges from deep suffering. Some prayers
are simply talking authentically to God about our suffering. Jesus

didn't hide his problems. We don't have to hide ours. Real prayer is real feelings expressed in real ways to a real God.

While our youngest son was hospitalized for thirty-two agonizing days after his appendix ruptured, he suffered greatly. The packing, unpacking, and repacking of infected wounds caused him to scream in agony. His cries were the most paralyzing and bewildering sounds I've ever heard. He was desperate. He was screaming for relief from the pain. When the time arrived for his dressing changes, everyone tensed up, and no one more than my son. As the specialist arrived at the assigned time, my son yelled out, "Oh God . . . Oh, God . . . Oh, God . . ." It was prayer. He was requesting intervention in the deepest way he has ever asked for anything.

Sometimes, on life's journey, only God's presence will do. He is the only one we can cry out to in our pain. No matter how many people are with us, there is something that only God can give and accomplish. Prayer is appealing for God to be God. Sometimes it's that simple. Psalm 23 opens with the words, "The LORD is my shepherd, I shall not be in want" (v. 1). As the shepherd's presence brings comfort and assurance to the sheep, the Shepherd of our souls fulfills the same role. God is with us, and he is with us in the agony.

Prayer is the soul's desire to communicate in an intimate and true way. God speaks and we listen. We speak and God listens. Soul-to-soul talk with God gives us a language with which we can speak fluently with God. We express our hearts to God, and God expresses his to us. If we hide our needs when we pray, our soul remains hidden to God and even to ourselves. Open, honest prayer is the best way to build an open relationship with God.

Sometimes Jesus spent the whole night talking to God (Luke 6:12). Can you imagine what this must have looked like? Can you see Jesus praying? Can you imagine his posture? Did he kneel, lie on his back, bury his face in his hands? Was he silent, or did he cry out? During sorrow and trial, even God in human flesh knew the best alternative was to pray.

## Your Soul Exercises

1. What "loud cries" have you uttered to God recently? Do you have any now?
2. Does it comfort you to know that Jesus prayed with passion? Why, or why not?
3. Does any physical prayer posture help when you're distressed? Why?

# 31

# Soul Freedom

We mostly spend lives conjugating three verbs: to want,
to have, and to do. Craving, clutching, and fussing . . . we
are kept in perpetual unrest.

EVELYN UNDERHILL

God made man simple; man's complex problems are of
his own devising.

ECCLESIASTES 7:29B JB

*O*ur culture encourages us to clamor for more. More stuff . . . more
toys . . . more involvement. Because we have so much, a container
and storage industry has grown into a thriving enterprise. We need
more space to store our stuff. Houses are now built with storage
rooms and walk-in closets. Not many decades ago simple wooden
wardrobes served as closets. An old armoire held the clothes.

A growing number of thoughtful people are pointing out the
benefits of simplicity. It sounds like a quaint notion, but we need to
practice simplicity. Simplicity seeks balance in a complex and complicated world. Simplicity values "less" in a culture that demands
"more" and "bigger." The world says, "More is more." The simplicity
alternative says, "Less is more." With less stuff, we carve out more
room for the soul to flourish.

If we're serious about soul care, we'll eventually reckon with
whether we'll decide for simplicity or continue to live with complexity. Practicing simplicity is a daily exercise that requires choosing
for the soul rather than choosing more things. Simplicity decides in
favor of the soul, allowing us to focus more on what matters—re-

lationships, inner growth, time with God, serving others—rather than devoting ourselves to things. We become more devoted to Jesus Christ.

Paul warns us that it's possible to lose our devotion to Christ. He says, "But I fear that somehow you will be led away from your *pure and simple devotion to Christ*" (2 Cor. 11:3 NLT, emphasis added). How is it that we have made devotion to Jesus so complicated? Our obsession with organization, information, and technology can smother the pure message of Jesus' love. His message promoted freedom for the soul that had long been held hostage by rules and regulations. The gospel of Jesus was good news, not more news.

Through simplicity we relinquish the "tyranny of the urgent" and live with the important. But how do we move in this direction? Practicing simplicity means asking, "What is the difference between needs and desires?" We apply the answer to this question in daily decisions. We think before purchasing and walk away from impulse. We de-clutter and set new priorities.

Practicing simplicity means courageously rescheduling time and agenda. We spend time on what nurtures the soul. A checkbook reveals what we value with our money, but PDAs and Day-Timers reveal how we value our time. When we practice simplicity, we learn to evaluate such issues as quality time versus quantity time.

Practicing simplicity means protecting the heart. We guard our heart "for it is the wellspring of life" (Prov. 4:23). We guard against things that thwart and distract us from what matters most. We detach from distractions and values that undermine the heart's pure and simple relationship with Jesus Christ. When we make space for simplicity in our lives, we eliminate the unnecessary. We unclutter life in order to understand what is necessary.

## Your Soul Exercises

1. When you envision a simpler life, what is it like?
2. How can you begin looking for ways to practice simplicity?
3. What does simple devotion to Jesus Christ mean?

# 32

# Sacred Reading

[The Bible] requires a willingness not just to read but to
be read, not just to master but to be mastered by words.

HENRI NOUWEN

You must crave pure spiritual milk so that you can grow
into the fullness of your salvation. Cry out for this nourishment as a baby cries for milk.

1 PETER 2:2 NLT

*L*iving words need to be read in an alive manner. A stale reading
of Scripture leads to a stale soul. Sacred reading involves reading
with the heart and not just the mind. We need to read with our spirit
open.

We're told that the journey from the mind to the heart is about
eighteen inches, yet for many this is the longest trip in the world.
Learning to read the Bible with the heart is a practice long subscribed
to by pilgrims who have valued reflection, meditation, and contemplation over speed, productivity, and results.

There are four simple steps to sacred reading. Each step utilizes
a Latin word that has a direct correlation in English. This ancient
practice is called *Lectio Divina,* which means "sacred reading."

- Step One: *Lectio*—the Latin for "reading aloud." Before reading the passage aloud, simply pray, "Lord Jesus Christ, speak
  to me." Read the passage slowly, asking the Lord to reveal what
  you need to understand and experience. Pause and consider
  what you have heard.

- Step Two: *Meditatio*—the Latin for "meditate." Rather than reading with speed to finish a short passage, read it again and again, "listening" for a particular word or phrase that impresses you. This repetition invites you to pause and "chew" on the chosen word or phrase. When the angel told Mary, the mother of Jesus, she would become the mother of the Messiah through a miraculous conception, she "pondered" what she had been told (Luke 2:19). Pondering is stopping, considering, and exploring the meaning in a deeper fashion.
- Step Three: *Oratio*—Latin for "pray." Pray the Scripture you have just read. Ask God to illuminate the verses that are just for you. In this step, ask God to touch and change you by the Word. Praying the Scriptures allows the words to become your words back to God in prayer.
- Step Four: *Contemplatio*—Latin for "contemplate." This is a wordless time when you sit in the presence of the living Word, allowing his presence to bring transformation. This wordless presence invites God to change the one who reads.

Many find it difficult to practice sacred reading because the heart is full of noise and distractions. This is understandable. To help, keep a pen and paper handy. Simply write down thoughts that come to mind like, "Call Jason," or "Instead of doing this, why don't you get busy and finish that project?" These are the demands of your conscience, but tell yourself that these tasks can be accomplished later. For now, you're tending to your soul, giving it life and nourishment.

A favorite quotation that has been ascribed to C. S. Lewis states, "We read to know that we are not alone." When we read the words of an author, in a way we become partners with that writer. We envision what he saw. We sense what she felt. We know what they know. By reading the Bible in a reflective way, we become God's companion. We linger in the presence of God, who breathes life into our souls and lights our paths.

## Your Soul Exercises

1. How do you usually read the Bible?
2. Which of these reading steps seems most beneficial for your soul?
3. Throughout the day, how can you reflect on what you've read?

## 33

# The Joy of Confession

The beginning of good works is the confession of evil
works. You do the truth and come to the light.

AUGUSTINE OF HIPPO

He who covers his sins will not prosper,
But whoever confesses and forsakes them will have
mercy.

PROVERBS 28:13 NKJV

*M*y son came to me quivering in fear. He had wrecked the family
car on one of his first outings as a new driver. It was a difficult
conversation. For my son, it involved owning up to a mistake that
damaged our car and the other driver's car. For me, it was the internal agony of another unexpected bill at a difficult time for our
family. As my son confessed his mistake, it was hard to focus because
my mind drifted to the question, "How are we ever going to pay for
this?" But at the end of our talk, my son said, "Dad, I feel so much
better. It really is good to just face the music and get it over."

To use my son's terminology, confession is facing the music.
Confession means facing the reality of what has happened with
the proper posture of the heart. A handbook of spiritual formation
defines confession as "the acknowledgement of individual and
corporate responsibility for one's actions and for growth in the
likeness to Christ under the guidance of the Holy Spirit."[1] When
my son acknowledged his actions, he faced the music of his heart.
He needed to get the feelings of guilt and remorse out of his soul.
The mood of confession centers on being penitent, contrite, or sorry.

Genuine confession carries the mood of confession converging with the words of confession.

My wife is quick to remind me when I ask for her forgiveness, "Steve, I need more than just your words." Normally, I want to confess, just to "get it over with," but that kind of attitude rarely gets me anywhere with my wife. She's really telling me that when I ask for her forgiveness, my heart needs to be contrite and match the words I'm speaking. The insincerity or shallowness of our words reveals the inner attitude of our soul when we confess.

David's words match his broken heart when he confesses, "When I kept silent, my bones wasted away through my groaning all day long. For day and night your hand was heavy upon me; my strength was sapped as in the heat of summer" (Ps. 32:3–4). David describes a physical reaction that is a symptom of not confessing sin. The mood matches the words.

Because they articulate a confession in which mood matches words, some psalms are referred to as penitential: 6; 38; 51; 102; 130; and 143. These psalms model how heartfelt confession looks, sounds, and feels.

Failing to own up to sin and refusing to seek forgiveness from God or others weighs down the soul with an unnecessary burden. John reminds us, "If we claim that we're free of sin, we're only fooling ourselves. A claim like that is errant nonsense. On the other hand, if we admit our sins—make a clean breast of them—he won't let us down; he'll be true to himself. He'll forgive our sins and purge us of all wrongdoing" (1 John 1:8–9 MSG).

Confession leads to forgiveness. By practicing confession, we own our sin and we open the door to resolution and joy.

## Your Soul Exercises

1. What does confession look like, feel like, and act like?
2. What is God saying in 1 John 1:8–9?
3. Is the need to confess surfacing in your soul?

34

# Listening for God

Listen and attend with the ear of your heart.

BENEDICT OF NURSIA

Obey My voice, and I will be your God, and you shall
be My people. And walk in all the ways that I have commanded you, that it may be well with you.

JEREMIAH 7:23 NKJV

*I*n the spiritual life, listening to God is essential. In the Old Testament, Moses commanded, "Hear, O Israel . . ." (Deut. 6:4a). In
order to hear, we must learn to listen. With noisy hearts within and
a screaming world without, listening to God isn't easy. We become
distracted and diverted from hearing God.

In addition, voices of shame and condemnation can drown out
the voice of love, which longs to speak tenderly to us. We are jeered
at by internal voices that can say, "This is a waste of time. God may
speak to others but he will never speak to you." The Accuser whis-
pers false statements into our hearts and consciences.

But we can hear God's voice, if we will listen. Jesus was aware of
our tendency to not listen. Consider his words:

- "He who has ears, let him hear" (Matt. 11:15; see also Mark
  4:9; Luke 8:8).
- "My sheep listen to My voice; I know them, and they follow
  Me" (John 10:27).
- "My mother and brothers are those who hear God's word and
  put it into practice" (Luke 8:21).

- "Mary has chosen what is better, and it will not be taken away
  from her" (Luke 10:42b). Jesus here is commending a woman,
  Mary, for listening intently to his teaching instead of focusing
  on meal preparations as her sister Martha.

God pleads with the children of Israel through the voice of his
prophet Isaiah when he says, "Listen, listen to me, and eat what is
good, and your soul will delight in the richest of fare. Give ear and
come to me; hear me, that your soul may live" (Isa. 55:2–3).

Samuel's story in 1 Samuel 3 offers insight into a young boy who
was willing to hear something from God. At first Samuel mistook
the voice in the middle of the night and went to his master, the priest
Eli. Then Eli realized that the boy was hearing the voice of the Lord.
As instructed by Eli, Samuel's prayer the next time God spoke was,
"Speak, LORD, for your servant is listening" (1 Sam. 3:9). That is an
invitation that each of us can offer to God.

We hear God in Scripture. The inspired pages of the Bible reveal
God's teaching and counsel. A. W. Tozer, the great preacher and
author, said, "I think a new world will arise out of the religious
mists when we approach our Bible with the idea that it is not only
a book which was once spoken, but a book which is now speaking.
The prophets habitually said, 'Thus saith the Lord.' They mean their
hearers to understand that God's speaking is in the continuous
present."[1]

Have you ever felt like God spoke to you? Think back to a time
when you had a clear, deep impression that you had heard something from God, perhaps through the counsel of a preacher, friend,
or even a stranger. How do you discern whether it is truly God who
is speaking?

Jesus reminds us, "He who belongs to God hears what God says"
(John 8:47). The soul that is immersed in Scripture can be quiet and
listen to what God is saying.

*Your Soul Exercises*
1. How does God speak today?
2. How do you experience God's voice?
3. What would it mean to begin your day with the prayer of Samuel: "Speak, LORD, for your servant is listening"?

## 35

# Fasting from Life

Fasting is the affirmation and experience of another world. Fasting is feasting.

DALLAS WILLARD

Instead of eating, I prayed.

PSALM 35:13 MSG

*F*asting is giving up one thing in order to focus temporarily on something more important. In the first century, it was a regular practice of Jews and the early Christians. Nearly every religion, in fact, holds to some form of abstaining from food for religious reasons. Jesus reminded his disciples that fasting is a personal and private exercise not to be publicly flaunted (Matt. 6:16–18). Jesus also said that the appropriate time for his disciples to fast would be after he had left them (Matt. 9:14–15). But Jesus did not offer details about the practice of fasting.

Jesus must have assumed that his followers would fast. He tells them in the Sermon on the Mount, "*When* you fast. . . ." not "*If* you fast . . ." (Matt. 6:17, emphasis added). Jesus viewed fasting as a specific act of abstaining from food for a specific period and an explicit reason. Jesus fasted for forty days, going into the wilderness to be alone with God and to engage in a spiritual battle with Satan. By abstaining from food, Jesus focused on God. When tempted to eat, Jesus replied, "It is written: 'Man does not live on bread alone, but on every word that comes from the mouth of God'" (Matt. 4:4). The fast from food allowed Jesus to "feast" in his relationship with his Father.

Jesus practiced fasting as a normal and expected spiritual exercise. But fasting is not just giving up food. It is engaging in prayer, solitude, and time with God. Fasting is giving up something in order to gain something more.

We can benefit from giving up things other than food to soulfully focus on our relationship with God. We live in a world dependent on technology, news, and information. We live in an age of consumerism, and we consume more than we need. Watch a television news channel, and see bold, colorful bits of news crawling across a banner at the bottom of the screen; the weather is offered in another small box with a different font and color, and the reporters are talking about something else that you need to know. It's information overload.

Have you ever considered fasting from information? We can become attached, even addicted to instant information. Fasting from technology, information, and being "wired" 24/7 can help us practice soul care. After intentionally becoming "unwired," our souls can feel more vital.

Have you considered fasting from unessential activities? Or have you ever considered fasting from living by the clock for a while? We live by the clock so much, managing time to get everything done and hurry here or there. Fasting from being preoccupied with time and schedules allows our obsession with time to wane, while our time with God can restore what has been depleted.

It is possible to allow the mind to relax by deciding to abstain from the paper, TV news, or e-mail for a time. Such acts of abstaining open up unstructured time to experience an unforced rhythm of life and grace. By giving ourselves personal margins, we offer God space to show up and make himself known.

*Your Soul Exercises*

1. Complete this sentence: "When I think of fasting, I think of . . ."
2. How could you fast from food, technology, or activities in the next week?
3. From what other things might you need to abstain occasionally?

# PART 6

# SOUL RETREAT

*Slowing Down in a Hurried World*

## 36

# Be Still and Know

How rare it is to find a soul quiet enough to hear God speak.

FRANÇOIS FÉNELON

In quietness and trust is your strength.

ISAIAH 30:15

*I* led a spiritual exercise in a church, asking people in the worship service to be still for five minutes. No music. No movement. Only being still and quiet. For many, it was difficult. For some, it seemed like forever.

After the service a woman said to me angrily, "I don't like it when you make us be still and quiet."

I asked, "Why is that?"

"When I'm quiet and still, I begin to have bad thoughts."

I couldn't let that go, so I asked, "What bad thoughts do you have when you are still?" I was unprepared for her honest and courageous response.

"When you made us be still, I started thinking of how unhappy I am, and how miserable I am in my marriage."

Busyness can numb us to a rattling emptiness in our souls. Often when we slow down, we have the opportunity to reflect and feel things that the speed of life doesn't allow us to acknowledge. Slowing down and being still can allow issues and questions to surface that we need to pay attention to and explore.

Children who play with inflated beach balls in the water use energy and force to keep the balls underneath the water. They push the balls down and sit on them. But eventually the balls pop up with an explosive force that shatters the water's calmness. The children fall off, squealing with delight.

In a similar way, problems that we push down eventually pop back up. We can suppress and deny issues for a while, but they can erupt to the surface with explosive and surprising force to dismantle lives. If we regularly take time to be still, it's possible we can deal incrementally with troublesome issues and diffuse their growing destructive power.

Practicing stillness for a few moments in a day allows us to feel, reflect, and experience peace. Paul describes this when he says, "You will experience God's peace, which is far more wonderful than the human mind can understand. His peace will guard your hearts and minds as you live in Christ" (Phil. 4:7 NLT).

The psalmist advises us to be still and know God (Ps. 46:10). The correlation between "being still" and "knowing" is interesting. Stillness evokes a confidence and realization that we can't gain otherwise. If we're not still, how can we ever experience what God wants to give us?

Practicing the art of being still is not difficult, but it is a discipline. This practice makes space for God to reveal something of himself or ourselves. Like learning to flex new spiritual muscles, we discover the life-giving aspects of a quiet stillness.

The Chinese word for *busy* is composed of two characters; one means "heart," and the other means "annihilation." When we are busy, our hearts deaden within us, and we can't hear the voice of divine love calling us to himself. Busyness kills the heart. Stillness is God's invitation: *Come. I want you to join me over here. Now, sit and wait for me. Yes, I am with you now.*

## Your Quiet Soul

1. Do you take time to be still? If so, what do you do?
2. What do (would) you like about being still? What do (would) you dislike?
3. How can you find time to be still without leaving your surroundings?

# Necessary Solitudes

*In solitude, where we are least alone.*

LORD BYRON

*But Jesus often withdrew to lonely places and prayed.*

LUKE 5:16

*A* few years ago, I attended a retreat with a well-known author and spiritual leader. The attendees were secluded in a monastery for three weeks. Being an extrovert, I felt like I was in a prison rather than on a spiritual retreat. My room was a monk's cell. While others embraced this new experience with gusto, I walked the grounds at night, wondering, *What was I thinking when I signed up for, much less paid for, this type of experience?* When the sky became dark, I walked down the hill to the gate. A wall completely surrounded the cloistered monastery grounds. No one could get in and, more problematic, I couldn't get out.

Then I spotted an alluring sign off in the distance. It was a life-giving sign: a green-and-white Starbucks logo. I could see tables filled with people drinking their mochas and lattes. Even the monastery coffee was lacking the kick I needed. So I figured out how to scale the monastery walls at night to visit that nearby sanctuary of caffeine. Rather than practice solitude, I escaped into what I thought was freedom.

Through the cloistered gates I could see something I wanted— something I needed. Starbucks became an escape from the spiritual retreat I'd planned and budgeted for—and desperately needed. But too much solitude offered me nothing at first. I thought I needed people more.

That retreat did teach me, however, about my true self. I had to face myself in solitude and couldn't hide behind people, laughter, and fun. In solitude, I had to be myself, accept myself, and be accepted by the God who loved me and called me his own.

Something happens in solitude that cannot happen in community. Something happens in solitude that does not happen at any other time. In solitude, we experience only ourselves. Community offers us companionship. With friends, we share our thoughts, dreams, and disappointments. Solitude extends the invitation only to God, and we share only with him.

Solitude invites us to experience the "oneness" that Jesus prayed for in John 17:22, when he said, "that they may be one as we are one."

There is a "giving up" when we practice solitude. We give up others and our dependency on them. We give up noise and our fascination with what we hear. We give up our tendencies to be trivial and obsessed with our manic pursuits. We learn to receive what only silence and aloneness can give.

When we practice solitude, we open our hearts and hands to finally receive. In our everyday work and life, we're tempted to make a fist to prove our point. Solitude relaxes the palms, prying them open to God's gifts. In these quiet moments, we are like a beggar who receives whatever is placed into his hands. In these moments of being "with God," we find that he becomes the Immanuel who is truly "with us."

After finally learning to practice solitude, I understand the tremendous benefit of unplugging from people and demands to bask in the presence of God alone. Solitude has offered me the healing and hope I've desired. Solitude replenishes the soul. This is why Jesus made solitude a regular and necessary part of his lifestyle and relationship with God. He detached from people so that he could attach to God. Solitude allows us to be stripped of others so that we can be covered with divine love.

## Your Quiet Soul

1. What do you need to let go of to open your heart and hands to God?
2. How can you practice solitude?
3. What did Jesus receive through solitude?

# True Retreat

It was an important day in my life when at last I understood that if [Jesus] needed forty days in the wilderness
at one point, I very likely could use three or four.

DALLAS WILLARD

After three days they found him in the temple courts,
sitting among the teachers, listening to them and asking
them questions.

LUKE 2:46

The pump at the gas station where I fill my car has four hoses attached to it. Four cars can fill up at one time. Each hose replenishes empty tanks from a reservoir of gas underneath the pavement.
But the soul is not like a gasoline pump. We cannot continually give.
We need to receive. We need to retreat.

Over the ages, spiritual retreats have been woven into the fabric of
the spiritual life. Religious festivals and special times of celebration
have been a rich part of the Judeo-Christian experience. Extended
times for pilgrimages and retreats are part of our spiritual heritage.
As our culture becomes busier and moves faster, I believe spiritual
retreats will emerge again as a necessity, not an option. How can we
be aware of the Father's voice speaking to us? How can we experience
the daily reality of Jesus' relentless pursuit of our wholeness? The
only way is to "pull away" and retreat with the Lord.

As a twelve-year-old boy, Jesus participated in a religious retreat
of sorts. His family joined the masses of Jews traveling to Jerusalem
to celebrate Passover. This holiday focused on remembering God's

faithfulness in the past. Jesus stayed longer in Jerusalem than did his parents. When Joseph and Mary discovered him missing, they set out on a panicked search. After three days they found him in the temple. Mary said to Jesus "Son, why have you treated us like this? Your father and I have been anxiously searching for you" (Luke 2:48). Jesus' reply reveals his soul's desire to focus on the spiritual life. Jesus asked, "Why were you looking for me? Didn't you know that I had to be here, *dealing with the things of my Father?*" (v. 49 MSG, emphasis added).

Jesus needed to engage in the things of God. He spent at least three days focusing on his heavenly Father. He drank in the water of God's Word, taught by devoted teachers. He engaged his heart and explored with his soul. He displayed exceptional understanding. Luke tells us, "Everyone who heard him was amazed at his understanding and his answers" (Luke 2:47). A retreat offers us the time to conduct the business of heaven, not just our own lives.

Jesus' time on his retreat was personal. This was a time for Jesus to delight himself in what nurtured his soul. Later, throughout his ministry, Jesus retreated. He spent an extended time of forty days in the wilderness, stayed overnight in the woods, got away by himself to pray and focus, and went mountain climbing with a few companions. These retreats enabled Jesus to deal with the things of God. He replenished his soul so his body could move ahead.

If Jesus needed to retreat, so do we. If we charge forward in our own strength, we deplete and eventually bankrupt the soul. Retreats can vary in length—one day; overnight; three days; a week; longer. Whatever the duration and content, retreats are not a luxury. They are a regular and necessary part of the Lord's lifestyle. And our goal is to be like him.

## *Your Quiet Soul*

1. When you think of a retreat, what do you envision?
2. What are the elements you need for a spiritual retreat?
3. How can you make an opportunity for a retreat in the next few months? How long? With whom? Where?

# Walking with God

Above all, do not lose your desire to walk. Every day I
walk myself into a state of well-being and walk away from
every illness. I have walked myself into my best thoughts,
and I know of no thought so burdensome that one cannot walk away from it.

SØREN KIERKEGAARD

Then the man and his wife heard the sound of the LORD
God as he was walking in the garden in the cool of the
day, and they hid from the LORD God among the trees of
the garden.

GENESIS 3:8

There's a trail not far from our home in Colorado. It reminds me of
what I imagine Eden to be like. It's perfect to walk in any season.
The trail offers a steady, gradual climb that a novice hiker who is
not in particularly good shape can accomplish. A spectacular vista
for hundreds of miles in all directions is a rich payoff. All along the
trail beauty abounds that transports me to another place altogether
in my soul.

A clear, babbling stream follows the trail, winding in and out of
forests of firs, scented pines, and aspen. In the distance, I can see
huge rock formations. Other rocks line the path, so one simply cannot get lost. Massive flat rocks, stacked like pancakes, stretch toward
the sky. Any weekend brings dozens of hikers to this place, but on a
weekday, I often walk alone on this trail of fulfillment and refresh-
ment. This is where I go to be with God, to walk with God.

This trail feels like a sacred, well-worn path for me. I go there often to be alone. But really, I am not alone. On a cool autumn afternoon, when the aspens are quaking with their golden hues and shades of yellow, I feel I could walk into the kind of scene described in *The Message* interpretation of Psalm 23:1–3:

> GOD, my shepherd!
>    I don't need a thing.
> You have bedded me down in lush meadows,
>    you find me quiet pools to drink from.
> True to your word,
>    you let me catch my breath
>    and send me in the right direction.

Knowing God walked through the paths of Eden helps me envision God walking beside me on this trail. God came in the "cool of the day" (Gen. 3:8) to stroll through Eden's lush gardens. God calls out to Adam and Eve as the seeking God from such a trail. On this trail, I often think of God looking for me, desiring my companionship. I am comforted in imagining that God is walking with me as he walked with Enoch, Noah, and others (Gen. 5:24; 6:9).

As nice as this woods-and-mountain walk can be, the experience can happen anywhere. Jesus walks with us as our souls' companion, whether we tread along dusty roads or paved highways. Just as he did with the disciples on the road to Emmaus, Jesus can walk with us today. However, the challenge for us is to recognize Jesus as he walks with us.

A walk with God affords a time when God draws close and joins his child. It is more than taking a walk on a physical path. It is an encounter and experience when we become aware of his presence, and this experience reminds us that we are not alone, that "God is with us."

The movement from being alone to be being with God is a life-giving step in soul care. To be with God is to enjoy his presence. The purpose is not an aerobic workout, but exercise to work out what's embedded in the soul. This soul exercise allows us to focus, grow quiet, be curious, pray, and hear God's voice. It's another way to experience Immanuel, God-with-us.

## Your Quiet Soul

1. What kind of walks do you prefer? Why?
2. How could you incorporate a time of closeness with God into your week?
3. How could such an activity care for your soul?

# Holy Thinking

A man's mind may be likened to a garden, which may be intelligently cultivated or allowed to run wild; but whether cultivated or neglected, it must and will bring forth.

JAMES ALLEN

It's best to stay in touch with both sides of an issue.

ECCLESIASTES 7:18 MSG

*O*pinions are like noses; everybody has one. But how do we know which opinion is right? How can we explore an issue without feeling swayed by personalities and authority figures so that we can know our own minds?

We can learn to think through issues and discern God's voice. Consider what King Solomon, the wisest person on earth said: "He who gets wisdom loves his own soul; he who cherishes understanding prospers" (Prov. 19:8). We practice soul care when we learn to make wise decisions and discover God's will in the process.

Learning to make wise decisions, that is, gaining wisdom, is different from being told what to think. Being told by an authority figure what to think is indoctrination; it's not thinking for yourself and gaining wisdom. Indoctrination is teaching someone to accept something as truth, uncritically. Discovering truth and gaining the valued prize of wisdom for ourselves comes from holy thinking. There's a big difference between being told what to think and being given the tools to explore for ourselves. A part of holy thinking begins when we accept that God's Spirit dwells within us. His

Spirit will guide and teach us so that we can trust the process of holy thinking, just as Jesus trusted and relied on his heavenly Father.

Mary, the mother of Jesus, engaged in holy thinking. After the shepherds described to Mary their encounter with the angel, "Mary treasured up all these things and pondered them in her heart" (Luke 2:19). Mary practiced two important elements of holy thinking. She treasured what had happened, and she pondered the meaning. She thought deeply about what the events meant and valued them like treasure. She pondered in response to God's actions, as opposed to immediately acting.

Mary also asked questions about what was happening to her. The traditional Christian teaching has been that—after Gabriel, the angel, told her she would become pregnant with God's Son—Mary just submitted. But we also see that she questioned Gabriel before she accepted (see Luke 1:26–38). Questioning should be part of the process of holy thinking, whether we hear something from the pastor, a TV evangelist, an Internet source, or a long-known friend. What are their motives and biases? What, exactly, are they saying? Does it ring true?

Quiet reflection—thinking through an issue or decision carefully—fills the soul with life-giving potential. It considers different sides and angles, perhaps the pros and cons of a decision, and gathers information from trustworthy people and sources. It sounds like a cliché, but God gave us our brain to use, especially for decision making.

How, then, do we practice and apply holy thinking?

"Start with GOD—the first step in learning is bowing down to GOD" (Prov. 1:7 MSG). Wisdom emerges from a God-orientation to life. By bowing to him, we ask for his help and guidance. We say, "God, I want your will, not my own."

Next, "you'll find wisdom on the lips of a person of insight" (Prov. 10:13 MSG). Wisdom exudes from wise people. Seek counsel from them. Don't wallow in a pool of ignorance, relying on the opinions of people you shouldn't trust.

Also consider that "plans fail for lack of counsel, but with many advisers they succeed" (Prov. 15:22). Wisdom often increases in the counsel of the many. Follow one line of thinking, and you could wind up isolated. But when you gain the different perspectives of those you trust, you can learn to trust holy thinking.

Holy thinking leads to health, wisdom, and freedom. It values our roles as God's beloved sons and daughters. Our Father loves us, and we in turn love our own souls. Part of soul care requires gaining courage through holy thinking to decide for ourselves what we really believe and then acting on our convictions.

## Your Quiet Soul

1. In your circle of friends, who has godly wisdom?
2. How can you treasure and ponder a circumstance you're facing?
3. How will you involve God in this decision?

# 41

# Journaling the Soul

If the God of the universe tells you something, you should write it down!

HENRY BLACKABY

Since I have investigated all the reports in close detail, starting from the story's beginning, I decided to write it all out for you, most honorable Theophilus, so you can know beyond the shadow of a doubt the reliability of what you were taught.

LUKE 1:3-4 MSG

*B*logs (personal notes written on online Web sites) are springing up all over the Internet. People around the world publish personal thoughts, reactions, and opinions for the world to read. It's estimated that as many as forty thousand personal cyberjournals start every day. So far that adds up to 8.5 million personal diaries on the Web. At the moment, blogging is a popular way to express our deepest thoughts. People want to believe that what they want to say matters.

Writing out thoughts isn't new, but today the Internet provides instant expression to anyone in the world who cares to connect and listen. Long before cyberspace, Christians such as Augustine of Hippo, Søren Kierkegaard, Blaise Pascal, and John Wesley wrote journals that for centuries have been read. Through these writings, the reader can explore the souls of people who were used by God in significant ways.

Prior to the printing press, stories were passed as parents and other elders of one generation taught them to children. Learned like that, people would not forget the insights, lessons, and events that had been indelibly imprinted in the history of their ancestors. God told the Israelites to remember their history so they wouldn't forget what he had done for them. Much soul shaping appears in the pages of the Old and New Testaments. Luke wrote his gospel and the book of Acts as a personal journal to record the life and teachings of Jesus Christ and the birth of the church.

Journals help us because, over time, they offer a road map about where we've been and where we're headed. David, the shepherd boy who became king, poured his soul into poems eventually collected in the book of Psalms. David's words can be our words. He rejoices of intimacy with God in one entry and in the next he complains that God seems far off. The courageous outpouring of one man's heart offers inspiration and even revelation into God's heart.

Journaling, then, works out what resides in the soul. A personal journal permits the soul to speak about what matters. Whether the pages are bounded by the Internet or bound in leather, personal reflections makes a journal significant.

I look back at pages written about each of my children, remembering how we studied options for their names, and why we chose the names we did. It takes some creativity to find first names that make the family name "Smith" sound significant.

I also wrote my impressions of their early years, noting interesting episodes that stood out as important at the time. I even recorded my prayers for their future spouses. I wanted their spouses to know that they were prayed for, that they were wanted, and that they would be highly valued in our family. I've recorded struggles and breakthroughs in my marriage. Career options and choices were painstakingly worked through in the journals, citing the pros and cons of the options facing me.

Looking back, I see patterns that motivated me to make the decisions I made. It's all valuable insight into understanding how God shapes my soul.

A journal can help us connect the dots and fill in gaps of our understanding. But most of all, a journal can tell the story of how God shapes us and reminds us of God's faithfulness. A journal records our attempts to answer the nagging question: *What is God up to in my life this week?*

## Your Quiet Soul

1. Have you read a journal or autobiography that impressed you? Why did it stand out?
2. What seems to be the biggest obstacle to journaling?
3. How can you make journaling a practice for your soul?

## 42

# Sabbath Rest

Because we do not rest we lose our way. . . . Poisoned by
the hypnotic belief that good things come only through
unceasing determination and tireless effort, we never
truly rest. And for want of rest, our lives are in danger.

WAYNE MULLER

Remember to observe the Sabbath day by keeping it
holy.

EXODUS 20:8 NLT

*O*ne Christmas my family gave me a global positioning system
(GPS) device, a handheld receiver that communicates with sat-
ellites to tell your exact location. We used this new toy on a number of fun family hikes, mapping our way back home using what we
learned on the GPS device.

The Sabbath offers us a soulful GPS. When used properly, it helps
us find the way home. Wayne Muller writes:

Our culture invariably supposes that action and accomplishment are better than rest, that doing something—anything—is better than doing nothing. We miss the compass
points that would show us where to go, we bypass the nourishment that would give us succor. We miss the quiet that
would give us wisdom. We miss the joy and love born of
effortless delight.[1]

Sabbath days help us find direction if we use them as God intended. I need Sundays more than any other day of the week. I feel things on the Sabbath that I don't feel when moving quickly. The Sabbath gives a more immediate sense of the Father's presence. Albert Schweitzer has said, "Do not let Sunday be taken from you. If your soul has no Sunday, it becomes an orphan."[2]

The soul needs a Sabbath. God's direction about Sabbath-keeping helps the soul survive and thrive. In the beginning God created the world in six days and on the seventh day he "rested" (Gen. 2:2). We have this picture of God resting in the sense of ceasing from creation as a model for life. God wrote a life rhythm that offers the opportunity to untether from things, people, and demands.

This sacred rhythm, demonstrated by God and practiced by Jesus, is a practical and definable way to practice soul care:

- Work, then rest.
- Engage, and then disengage.
- Get involved, and then get uninvolved.
- Tether yourself to responsibilities, goals, and agendas, then untether.

God established a rhythm to life that goes, six days to work and one day of rest. It is a six-to-one rhythm, not five to one or fourteen to one.

The word transliterated into English as a noun, *Sabbath*, comes from a Hebrew verb that has the literal root meaning "cease." On a Sabbath, we cease. We do not continue at the same speed of the other days. On the other days we strive, toil, and endure. Sunday is to be different, for it was set aside at the start of church history as the Christian Sabbath because it marks the day of Christ's resurrection. To practice a soul's Sabbath requires a different perspective than our culture values. Achieving and busyness are not applauded on the Sabbath. Rest is affirmed and valued. Work waits for tomorrow. Something wonderful happens deep inside when we practice the Sabbath.

We enter a danger zone when we do not cease from work and the demands of others. The soul is not an animal to be herded, driven, and laden. Our souls bear the image of God and reflect the sacred. Jesus is Lord of the Sabbath (Matt. 12:8; Mark 2:28; Luke 6:5) and told us that it was made for us (Mark 2:27).

This significant day encourages us to manage time in a different way. Except for times of worship, we aren't as pressured to be anywhere or to do anything on a strict schedule. We leave unnecessary things "undone" until the Sabbath is over. When we return to our work and worries, we feel refreshed, better able to manage the onslaught.

Because this particular day is kept, certain activities become rituals. We keep a commitment to family or community. Perhaps close friends come for dinner, or we visit them. We share being together. Meals during the week are more time conscious. A Sabbath meal can be a lingering experience of food and fellowship. We may spend time reading, napping, praying, talking—whatever slows us down and touches the soul.

"Our culture invariably supposes that action and accomplishment are better than rest, that doing something—anything—is better than doing nothing,"[3] Muller observes. As a result, it takes discipline to follow the pattern of God's day of rest. But when we keep the Sabbath, we value what God values.

### *Your Quiet Soul*

1. Was Sabbath observed in your childhood home? If so, how?
2. Have you treated the Sabbath differently at various stages in your lifetime?
3. What is a restful Sabbath day for you?

# PART 7

# SOUL GEOGRAPHY

*Exploring Life's Spiritual Destinations*

# 43

# Geography of the Soul

People are moved to wonder by mountain peaks, by vast waves of the sea, by broad waterfalls on rivers, by the all-embracing extent of the ocean, by the revolutions of the stars. But in themselves they are uninterested.

AUGUSTINE OF HIPPO

For since the creation of the world God's invisible qualities—his eternal power and divine nature—have been clearly seen, being understood from what has been made.

ROMANS 1:20

Run your hand along some topographical maps, and you'll feel the "earth's surfaces." Ridges protrude, indicating mountain ranges. Indentations represent deep oceans and placid lakes. Wavy patterns reveal smooth plains and piedmont. The contoured map represents the surface, the outer world. Our inner world, the invisible soul, also contains varied surfaces like the terrain of a topographical map. Like the ocean depths or mountain peaks, each soul has places that are often unexplored. The outer geography of the world is a helpful analogy in exploring the inner territory of a person.

In the soul, smoothed-out and well-worn places are created by life experiences. Less-traveled paths cross jagged, more dangerous places. To explore soul geography is to embark on a spiritual pilgrimage, venturing into depths of buried passion and wounds, where dream, visions, love, and hatred are birthed. It is an incomparable journey to explore the depths and heights of the soul, and we should feel awed by our inner landscape. God in the Holy Spirit resides deep within the Christian's soul. Knowing that God is within us helps us embrace our souls as sacred ground.

Jesus used the imagery of inner geography in his parable about seed scattered over four kinds of soils (Mark 4:1–20). His horticulture lesson about the spiritual life described various kinds of people, characterized by hardened, rocky, thorny, and good soils. When a farmer scattered seeds, each type of soil produced a different growth pattern but only one had a plentiful harvest. Reflecting on this story, we can ask, *What kind of soil is inside of me? How can I cultivate fertile soil to grow my faith? What thorns are choking the life out of me?* Jesus looked to stories of mountains and seas to teach us about God, faith, and life. He used the physical world to explain inner geography. These geographic journeys expand our understanding of the vast kingdom of God.

Three of Jesus' disciples accompanied him to the summit of a mountain where they experienced a soul-quaking view of what Jesus is like in glory. Within this "mountaintop experience," they heard the voice of God.

During Jesus' forty days in the wilderness, he encountered the Father, Satan, and his own human soul, and worked through temptations we all face in some fashion. In the cities, Jesus was moved to weep over the needs of throngs of people. At such times, Jesus would slip away to hilltops and gardens where he had intimate encounters with God the Father.

Matthew, Mark, Luke, and John show Jesus moving from one geographical setting to another. In each, something transformational happened. These geographical and environmental metaphors help us discern our own inner soul geography. The mountains offer us a sense of wonder, thrill, and ecstasy. The valley is a place of sadness and sometimes bewilderment. The desert can be stagnating or it can allow growth in contemplative solitude. Each place offers a different experience, but all are part of the journey of the soul. We grow both through the thrill of mountaintops and the despair of valleys. Sometimes we linger longer in the desert than we would ever want.

How will we handle the various places into which we are invited or thrown?

Jesus' lessons and experiences teach us how to care for our souls in each setting. We can see what Jesus did and how he responded. The trails that Jesus blazed to the mountaintops and valley floors lead us to look to our own soul needs in comparable life experiences.

Exploring the inner geography of the soul shows twists and turns, the ruts and rocks. It helps avoid stumbling and wandering from the path, for us and for those sharing our path.

## Your Soul Geography

1. What terrain compares to your soul's condition?
2. What terrain of your soul seems well known?
3. What places in your soul have gone unexplored?

# Up the Mountain

Climb the mountains and get their good tidings. Nature's
peace will flow into you as sunshine flows into trees. The
winds will blow their own freshness into you . . . while
cares will drop off like autumn leaves.

JOHN MUIR

Jesus . . . went up onto a mountain.

LUKE 9:28

*L*iving near the base of Pikes Peak, I have the opportunity to see
scores of people ascend "America's Mountain" each day. At the
trailhead, young and old hikers begin a trek to the summit, 14,110
feet above sea level. People climb for the adventure, because a significant mountain invites us to climb.

Mountains have always drawn pilgrims in search of a soul respite.
Places that are high and removed entice those in search of emotions
that standing on the heights can give. Peaks and snowy pinnacles
promise the reward of grandeur for the one who climbs. Mountains
always call the soul to get away from the distractions. As people ascend, cares seem to fall off and our burdens become lighter. Pilgrims
who were headed to Jerusalem's mountain for festivals would sing
psalms—specifically Psalms 120–134, called Psalms of Ascent—to
remind them of their hearts' true destination: the presence of God.

We recognize in mountains the majesty and strength of God. The
psalmist cries out as he gazes up, "I look up to the mountains; does
my strength come from mountains? No, my strength comes from

GOD, who made heaven, and earth, and mountains" (Ps. 121:1–2 MSG). Huge, big, invincible mountains can remind us of our incomparable God.

Jesus went to mountains to pray (Luke 6:12) and to hear from God (9:28). Some of the peaks he climbed were over nine thousand feet above sea level. One mountain in particular became more of a journey of encounter. For Jesus and his climbing companions, the mountain was a sanctuary where they worshiped God and had unforgettable times with him. On the mountain of transfiguration, mystery engulfed them, and they saw Jesus for who he really is.

Have you ever had a "mountaintop experience"? Even the phrase implies that, somehow and in some specific way, one feels closer to God. After the journey up, you understand the necessity of that long, arduous ascent on the winding trail—for at the top is the fulfillment of what was hoped for all the way up. There is a sacred sense of God being there. Things can be seen more clearly in the thinness and clearness of the mountaintop experience.

### Your Soul Geography

1. What do mountains mean to you?
2. What are positive images of mountains that could translate to your spiritual life?
3. What mountaintop experiences can you recall in your walk with God?

# 45

## Sacred Waters

A river is the most human and companionable of all in-
animate things. It has a life, a character, a voice of its
own, and is as full of good fellowship as a sugar-maple
is of sap. It can talk in various tones, loud or low, and of
many subjects grave and gay. . . . For real company and
friendship, there is nothing outside of the animal kingdom that is comparable to a river.

HENRY VAN DYKE

Mightier than the thunder of the great waters,
mightier than the breakers of the sea—
the LORD on high is mighty.

PSALM 93:4

Raging storm waters recently flooded the streams around our city.
Thunderstorms produced torrential rain that caused flash flood-
ing. Two small boys were swept away while wading in a rising stream.
The rushing water meant danger, but the boys were plucked from the
jaws of death by rescuers and had a new opportunity to live.

The Bible uses water, whether raging in fury or quiet and still, to
teach soulful lessons about God's character and attributes. Throughout Scripture, God uses water to reveal his ability to deliver us and
save us from peril. Isaiah reminds us of God's promise to deliver us
when we read, "When you pass through the waters, I will be with
you; and when you pass through the rivers, they will not sweep over
you" (Isa. 43:2). The children of Israel passed through the parted
waters of the Red Sea and were delivered from bondage (Exod. 14).

As a result, they were saved from annihilation. Jesus demonstrated his ability as God to calm raging seas when the disciples were panic stricken (Mark 4:35–41). He reached out to rescue Peter after Peter tried to walk on water (Matt. 14:22–33). Water also is used in Scripture to symbolize God's cleansing and grace in offering a new beginning. The great flood in Noah's day brought a cleansing judgment from God (Gen. 6–8). Ezekiel uses a water metaphor to describe the limitless depths of God's love (Ezek. 47). The water of baptism, from John's baptism of repentance (Matt. 3; Mark 1) through the baptism practiced in the church, is an important image. Baptism symbolizes new life and connection to God's family.

In terms of stress, you may feel you are neck deep in water right now. Work can overwhelm, and difficult relationships can make us feel as if we are sinking. Financial storms weigh us down. Chaotic storm waters of stress can overtake us and those we love. When the waters threaten, we pray and want the danger to recede so that we can breathe freely again. If the water keeps rising past our noses, we may feel that we are about to drown.

Countless others before us have gotten soul soaked and prayed in panic. Then something happens. God shows up, and in some way that may be unexpected, we feel the water receding. We sing and shout hallelujahs! We dance for joy because of our deliverance. We are saved—*again!*

Some truly think that they should be able to escape life perils because they decide to follow Jesus. But we soon learn that God is able to deliver from perils. He takes us through the flood waters in life more often than around them. Sitting in the swamped boats of our own efforts, we may wonder whether we're going to sink. With water rising all around, we muster the strength to cry out to God. Then, whatever the outcome, the winds and storm in us subside. We may suffer loss, but God has shown himself sufficient yet again.

Rising water and swamped boats are one way God builds our faith and strengthens our trust. We should not easily forget that God has been delivering his people since the beginning of human history.

Do it again, God, for me today.

## *Your Soul Geography*

1. What storm is happening in or near you?
2. What swamps your boat?
3. Do you need protection from a raging storm? Try writing a prayer asking for deliverance and think what you would write in praise to God for his deliverance.

# In the Valley

One sees great things from the valley, only small things from the peak.

G. K. CHESTERTON

Even when I walk
through the dark valley of death,
I will not be afraid,
for you are close beside me.

PSALM 23:4 NLT

*I* accompanied a group of high school seniors on a backpacking trip into the mountains. After a rigorous day of hiking uphill, we reached our campsite, which overlooked the valley floor. That evening we warmed ourselves by a campfire. The glittering stars dotted the heavenly canopy as we lay on our backs. One of the guys spoke for all of us when he said, "Let's stay up here forever. I don't want to ever go down."

Most of us long to stay on the mountain. The descent into the valley can be challenging, and we feel wobbly and unsteady. Walking through what Psalm 23:4 calls "the valley of the shadow of death" is painful and frightening. We lose perspective and the feeling of security that should be there with faith. Spiraling down into the valley is not an adventure of choice. It comes with sudden failure or tragedy. Valleys await, chosen or not, on each person's pilgrimage.

Entering a valley within your soul comes with a realization that something long desired or possessed is lost. Certainly you are not up where you can look out, smell the air, and enjoy the vista. Instead, canyon walls of stone surround you, preventing an easy escape.

The loss of a job, the loss of a relationship, the loss of status or power—practically speaking, the loss of almost anything—can usher a person very quickly into a valley in the soul. How we got there isn't as important as what we'll do at the bottom.

Valley times of the soul can be unpredictable. We don't know what is ahead. Valleys are experienced, not escaped. We endure the lows, feel the agony, and hope for a way out. These are times of aloneness, yet for those in Christ, the awareness of our traveling companion makes all the difference. Valleys of the soul feel lonely. Yet, even in the midst of the feeling, we realize that we are not alone. This is precisely what we learn in a valley time.

That God has promised his presence in the valleys of life is a transforming truth. He has said that he will never leave us or forsake us (Heb. 13:5). Even in times of the lowest despair, his rod and staff of Psalm 23 gently nudge us, assuage the fear and loneliness, and remind us that he is walking with us through the darkness.

## Your Soul Geography

1. What are valley times like for you?
2. What lessons have you learned in the valley times that you would have missed on the mountaintop?
3. What help is needed by someone who has experienced a prolonged valley time?

# The Wilderness

Wilderness is at the root of our lives. It is the home, the reunion we yearn for when we watch a sunset and feel heartache. . . . It is the reason we make heroes of our explorers and astronauts.

MARY JEAN PORTER

Therefore, behold, I will allure her, and bring her into the wilderness, and speak comfortably unto her.

HOSEA 2:14 KJV

*S*everal years ago, our family went camping in several of America's national forests. We longed to enter miles of wild beauty to find rest. In these protected forests we encountered wilderness beauty that healed our weary hearts. We regained perspective and returned to life. We emerged from those forests with life inside because God had met us there. The trip was more than a vacation; it was a soulful retreat.

The wilderness is a vast, uncultivated, uninhabited region. Here beauty abounds. Glory is rampant. But so is danger. The word *wilderness* contains the word *wild*, implying that the wilderness is neither tame nor civil. You might lie on unspoiled carpets of flowers in dozens of colors, or you might see a grizzly bear or a mountain lion. Sheltering within the forest, spreading across pristine meadows and glacier lakes, the wilderness stretches on and on. Such territory invites adventure, and offers an unparalleled escape into the virgin unknown.

A person feels very small in the vastness of an exquisite beauty that must be like Eden before the Fall. How can wildness, perfection, peace, and astonishment join in such a place? The soul knows. The wilderness within is just such a place of wonder and wildness, splendor and starkness, glory and ruin. Embedded within is the mysterious wilderness of the human soul.

The soul is like a wilderness area that can lead a person to scale great heights and do unspeakable things. Lying concealed within us is a vast territory of the spiritual domain. The soul, like the wilderness, is often unknown and unexplored.

In the wilderness, there are havens of solitude and paths of peace. When you walk into a backwoods area, you feel as if you are walking into God's sanctuary. The vastness can be alarming, feeling almost dangerous. You might get lost if you wander too far.

In *Les Misérables*, Victor Hugo speaks of one spectacle that is grander than the sea or the sky. This grandest spectacle is the soul. Creator-awareness is found in this vast domain. The human person is "fearfully and wonderfully made . . . my soul knows it very well" (Ps. 139:14 NASB). These fearful and wonderful characteristics of the human soul have been subjects of religions, philosophies, poems, and songs, but a sense of them lies naturally within the soul.

To explore our own souls, is an expedition into a wilderness filled with adventure, beauty, and danger. Representatives of every time, part of the world, and religion have tried to adequately describe this land of the inner person. Theologians try to articulate what the soul is. Philosophers argue its definition. Scientists attempt an analysis. But within our flesh and bones lies the vast and unspeakable, for here the God of creation takes up residency and dwells within.

The territory of the soul is a place of breathtaking beauty and unparalleled adventure. It is a place that juxtaposes beauty and wildness, grace and glory, but in the Christian as temple of the Holy Spirit it is also sacred (1 Cor. 3:16). Thus, with our soul we magnify the Lord and bless him (Pss. 34:2–3; 103:1–5). All that is within us yearns to bless the God who made us.

## Your Soul Geography

1. In what ways is your soul a wilderness?
2. What parts of your soul lie unexplored?
3. David says we should let all that is within us bless his holy name (Ps. 103:1). How might you bless the Lord today?

# Desert Sanctuary

And wherever you go, by land or by sea, you shall not forget that which you saw not but rather felt—the desolation and the silence of the desert.

JOHN C. VAN DYKE

O God, you are my God,
earnestly I seek you;
my soul thirsts for you,
my body longs for you,
in a dry and weary land
where there is no water.

PSALM 63:1

The desert is a place of paradox, where beauty is stark and arid. The spiritual desert is where pilgrims visit and linger on the journey. Here, the parched landscape thirsts for God alone, but God can seem distant or silent. The scorching desert journey tests the endurance. One doesn't thrive in such a place.

The desert, though, also is a place of transformation. One adapts or dies in the desert times of life. The soul changes in the desert. Reduced to the essence of life or death, the healthy soul emerges a champion. Like a shriveled flower, an alive soul can revive with just a drop of water. In the desert, tears are a life-restoring liquid. The desert is, indeed, a strange place.

During many years in the desert, Abraham experienced a transformation that prepared him to be father of many nations. The Israelites sojourned in the desert wilderness for forty years in anticipation of a land that would fulfill their deepest longings and God's promise. David fled to the desert to hide from Saul, who was pursuing him to kill him. In the desert, David wrote psalms of hope and comfort to all those who have been forced into the desert or fled there for their own reasons. Elijah spent forty days in a desert where the desolate conditions mirrored those of his barren soul. While there, Elijah learned to listen to God, and he emerged a transformed man. After Paul was converted to Christ, he went to the desert for three years. The desert became a place of profound change.

The desert does not always have to be feared or dreaded, because transformation happens in such places. We've been told that solitude is the furnace of transformation, and indeed change happens in authentic ways when there is no way of escape or any place to hide. Jesus chose a thirty-five- by fifteen-mile stretch of desert as a place of final preparation at the start of his public ministry (Matt. 4:1–11 and parallels). In that lonely place, Jesus met with the Father, came face to face with the Evil One, and emerged resolved to do the work he was called to do.

Not all deserts look alike. Some are huge, as much land mass as some entire continents. Some can be crossed by car in a few hours. Nor are all deserts of the soul the same. Some stretch to the horizons, offering no hope of escape. Some desert times are brief and are passed through with only minor singeing from the scorching heat.

For many, the desert is a place of questions. Our souls thirst for answers, and we feel that unless we get the answers, we will not survive. Where are you, God? Why are you so far away? I don't feel close to you anymore. What happened? The desert can strip the soul to its essence, revealing what matters most. Survival is the only reality we know. Because little distracts us, the desert becomes a sanctuary for the soul to pray as is nowhere else. The soul's thirst is transformed into groans and translated into earnest prayers. Nothing matters more in the desert than to find the relief for which the soul yearns. We wait and thirst, until the sweet relief of God comes. Through this process we can find transformation. Our spiritual dryness and the thirst of our parched souls is slaked through our soul's yearning for what matters most, God's presence deep within.

## Your Soul Geography

1. How would you describe a spiritually dry time in your life?
2. How does a desert time change a person?
3. How does God's presence bring relief in your desert times?

# Soul and the City

What is the city but the people?

WILLIAM SHAKESPEARE

O Jerusalem, Jerusalem, you who kill the prophets and stone those sent to you, how often I have longed to gather your children together, as a hen gathers her chicks under her wings, but you were not willing!

LUKE 13:34

Cities matter to God. Jerusalem moved Jesus' heart when he viewed it from a distance. His words about Jerusalem reveal a passion to embrace, rather than shun, the city. Inside the city were thousands of people, each significant and each in need of his message. Jesus was moved by the city because people matter to God, and the city is where people dwell in large numbers.

As much as the natural world displays the beauty of God's handiwork, cities reveal the deep compassion of God's heart. Cities are where people live and work, where they forge relationships and practice their faith. Within the city, rival religions, competing values, and clashing cultures interact. Yet in the midst of such commotion, faith grows.

No doubt, there is a role for the monastery and the soul within it. But a different kind of courage is needed to survive and thrive in the city. Urban areas mark the spirit and soul with culture and civilization.

Much of the history of our faith unfolded in such towns and cities as Jericho, Nineveh, Dan, Babylon, Bethlehem, and Jerusalem. In the alleys and streets, the faith of our Jewish and early Christian ancestors took root, as people met to worship. Pleased with the worship of his people, God placed his magnificent temple in the middle of a city, a place where praise would be continually offered.

Jesus ministered within and without Jerusalem's city gates. In the hub of the city, Jesus found liberals and conservatives, those who longed for the strict ways and those who begged for something new. King Herod the Great transformed Jerusalem into an amazing city before his death, which came soon after Jesus was born. Herod built aqueducts and monumental public works and palaces. The wondrous buildings, especially the Jewish temple, could be seen from the Mount of Olives, a high point near the city. The temple was built at the highest point of the city, so no one could miss it. The temple was central to the Jewish faith, and Jesus, being a Jew, frequented this place. In the splendor of the temple, his message could be preached effectively.

The city is a crossroad of ideas, religions, and politics. The Christian faith does not teach that we must flee from people and escape the world. The good news of Jesus is for the person on the city streets and in the marketplace. Our faith embraces urban concerns and expresses compassion for the poor inside the city's walls. We concern ourselves with government and leadership, as well as integrity in the marketplace. In cities and villages, Jesus' message was always the same.

The apostle Paul spread the gospel in a strategic city-to-city missions plan that contributed to the dramatic growth of the early church. Whether in Corinth or Ephesus, Paul knew that diverse people all needed the same good news. People gathered in the cities, but they also left to trade, work, and travel to other places, and this network brought about the rapid expansion of the New Testament church.

Jesus loved Jerusalem. He felt compassion for those within its gates. No matter how large the place where you live, the message of Jesus is for those people.

## Your Soul Geography

1. Do you like city life? Why, or why not?
2. How does an urban dweller practice soul care?
3. What advantages does city life offer to a seeking soul?

# PART 8

# SOUL SENSE

*Nurturing the Soul with the Senses*

# Ministers to the Soul

The five senses are the ministers of the Soul.

LEONARDO DA VINCI

From the very first day, we were there, taking it all in—we *heard* it with our own ears, *saw* it with our own eyes, verified it with our own *hands*. The Word of Life appeared right before our eyes; we saw it happen! And now we're telling you in most sober prose that what we witnessed was, incredibly, this: The infinite Life of God himself took shape before us.

1 JOHN 1:1–2 MSG (EMPHASIS ADDED)

God equipped us with five incredible senses with which we experience life and the world around us. Through these senses, we experience or detect the world around us. We see. We touch. We hear. We smell. We taste. Sense experience deepens our experience with God in ways that go beyond our intellect. Paul described it as, "to know [God's] love that surpasses knowledge" (Eph. 3:19).

The five senses take in information that develops our understanding of the world and God. These God-given senses increase our enjoyment of the abundant life that Jesus promised. We feel the peace that transcends all understanding in our bodies as well as our emotions, a sense of well-being beyond all comprehension. The mind does not understand. The senses teach life lessons.

By touching a hot flame, we learn to be careful. The smell of an apple pie baking in the oven makes us salivate. The sight of a sunset can stop that endless chatter in our minds and turn our hearts toward

God. Listening to a moving piece of music stirs us. The senses help us experience life within our souls.

With eyes we see, and others see us. It has been said that the eyes are the window of the soul. Have you ever felt uncomfortable when someone wouldn't make eye contact with you? Have you experienced intimacy when a friend looks you in the eye as he or she listens? Teachers can often look into a student's eyes and know whether the pupil is speaking the truth. And what a gift it is to use our eyes to take in works of art and nature.

We touch and feel the touch of others. That hug or touch on the arm in a time of crisis helps us feel less alone. We experience love, intimacy, and gentleness. Through a hug at the end of a long day, my wife knows if I am tense or stressed by work.

We listen and hear with the ears, and others hear and listen to us. We can distinguish moods, attitudes, and subtleties in the tone of voice. As my wife reminds me, "Steve, it's not what you say; it's how you say it that matters."

With the nose, we smell the fragrances. Appetites are stirred by the barbecue grill smoking in the yard. With tongues, we taste the sweetness and sourness of food. We appreciate and enjoy a ripe strawberry in the early summer and the taste of freshly brewed coffee in the early morning.

Aren't you glad that God gave senses that evoke gratitude? Let us "taste and see that the LORD is good" (Ps. 34:8), David urged. We are the "aroma of Christ" (2 Cor. 2:15). We can see the "invisible qualities—his eternal power and divine nature" in creation (Rom. 1:20).

Jesus touched people, and they were healed. He blessed the children by touching them and holding them on his lap. The sounds of the lute and the lyre are a foundation for worship as those gathered sing psalms, hymns, and spiritual songs. Music teaches the magnificence of God. We drink the cup and eat the bread, and our soul is satisfied beyond the taste experience of grapes and wheat.

This is how our senses help minister to our souls in deep and meaningful ways. We eat a meal with friends, and it feels like we have arrived at home. A father touches his daughter's shoulder in church or hugs his son after a baseball game, and the touch becomes more than a touch.

Often, living a sensory life has been judged harshly. And, yes, it is easy to encounter sin through our senses and thus misuse and abuse their sacred purpose as intended by God. Each of our senses has a sacred and evil side, and it is up to each of us to foster the sacred.

Jesus taught us to sharpen our senses by seeking to do God's will in all things. Jesus undoubtedly enjoyed, for example, the fragrance of spices in the oils that Mary lavished upon him. While some thought this experience a waste of time and resources, Jesus commended Mary for her act.

Jesus used the sight of birds to teach us not to worry. He enjoyed wine at weddings and even at feasts with tax collectors. He heard cries of the needy and was moved. Jesus appealed to our minds to look at the birds and flowers and see deeper truths.

Experiencing God through the senses is a wonderful way to practice care of the soul. Consider how you can practice soul care by engaging all of your senses.

### Your Soul Sense

1. Which is your favorite sense? Why?
2. Through which sense do you most often experience God?
3. How do you feel about multisensory worship experiences, using candles, drama, technology, musical instruments, video, art, poetry, and sculpture?

# The Glory of Sight

The eyes are the gateway to the soul.

HERMAN MELVILLE

They approached Philip, who was from Bethsaida in
Galilee: "Sir, we want to see Jesus. Can you help us?"

JOHN 12:21 MSG

On a Sunday hike a few years ago my family climbed to the top of
some red rocks and scaled the ridges so we could enjoy the beauty
and majesty of snowcapped peaks and a radiant blue sky. Evergreen
trees framed the fantastic view. One of my sons exclaimed, "Dad,
this is the most beautiful scene I've ever seen. God is here with us."
He had sharpened his awareness of God's presence in creation. His
eyes helped him see with his heart a deep mystery of the soul.

Eyes help us discover and encounter God. We seek to see the
invisible. Looking at the world shows God's eternal power (Rom.
1:20). Creation reveals the drama and power of a God who created
the world, and we get to behold it. As a visual artist, photographer
Ric Ergenbright observes that "if all Scripture were lost, we could
still know something of His character by carefully studying the work
of His hands. From its tiniest detail to its most majestic vistas, the
whole earth points us to the sovereign God of the Bible."[1]

Eyes receive the message of God's majesty so that the soul can
translate that information and show us the beauty, majesty, awe, and
splendor of God. When we see glory in nature, we see something
deeper and beyond the object to the Artist who crafted it. We see the
great mountains and feel small. We gaze at columbine growing wild

on the trail and wonder at the exquisite detail of its petals and design. We are moved to deep wonder as a newborn baby emerges from
the womb. David, the poet worshiper, said, "When I consider Your
heavens, the work of Your fingers, the moon and the stars, which
You have ordained, what is man that You are mindful of him, and
the son of man that You visit him?" (Ps. 8:3–4 NKJV). Physical eyes
stir response in the soul.

Our eyes lead us to marvel, contemplate, and stop to worship the
Creator. A stunning sunset at the coast makes us pause. A snowy
mountain range in winter moves us to consider God's greatness and
splendor. We see glory, and we pause to ponder. This is what the eyes
do. They give us information that translates to insight deep within
our souls, which in turn reveal more than the physical eyes can. Paul
prayed "that the eyes of your heart may be enlightened" (Eph. 1:18a).
The heart can see spiritual truth, while the physical eyes interpret
the visible world around us.

Our eyes also foster troubling challenges, such as lust, envy, and
covetousness. We translate what we see into our hearts. Desires come
alive. Passion ignites. Longings are stirred. God allows us to focus
on what brings life, or to choose what erodes the soul. We can read
words of life to which the heart will respond. It's our responsibility
to fix our eyes and minds on what will bring life. Paul reminds us,
"whatever is true, whatever is noble, whatever is right, whatever is
pure, whatever is lovely, whatever is admirable—if anything is excel-
lent or praiseworthy—think about such things" (Phil. 4:8).

It's hard to focus attention on what God is doing. We are easily distracted, and the soul doesn't always have 20/20 vision. By the
time I turned forty, it was evident that I couldn't see as well. People
at church joked about my tendency to hold my Bible almost at arm's
length when I read. I needed glasses to see more clearly. The soul also
can lose focus, but glasses won't fix the problem. It can be hard to see
what God is doing in us, and the speed at which we live makes what
God is doing seem a passing blur. The soul loses focus and perspective. We take so many wonders for granted as we rush by, missing
countless opportunities to experience God in our midst.

Whether it was the visual lesson of the mustard seed or the white-caps on the stormy sea, Jesus invited followers to witness visually what God is doing. With eyes, we experience a depth of understanding that offers insight and comfort. Nothing speaks to our souls with as much force as pain and beauty. Pain stops us in our tracks with blunt force trauma; beauty soothes and ministers.

Beauty ushers us into places of the soul that breathe life, inspiration, and awe. Seeing beauty, we hear the voice of the God who inspired it. Beauty turns our eyes toward Jesus.

## Your Soul Sense

1. What are your favorite places to see the works of God? How does natural beauty affect you?
2. The Bible links spiritual and physical blindness. Was there a time when God opened the eyes of your understanding?
3. What does it mean that "we live by faith, not by sight" (2 Cor. 5:7)?

## 52

# The Wonder of Sound

This is my Father's world,
And to my listening ears
All nature sings, and round me rings
The music of the spheres.

MALTBIE D. BABCOCK

Obey My voice, and I will be your God, and you shall
be My people. And walk in all the ways that I have commanded you, that it may be well with you.

JEREMIAH 7:23 NKJV

Counseling a couple about their marriage, I became frustrated. The
husband was not listening to his wife. She shared what she feared
were indications of their dying love. At one point the husband put
his hands over his ears. I asked what he was doing, he answered, "I
simply can't hear her anymore." I asked him to stop and pray that
God would help him grow his ears to become like the big, floppy
ears of an elephant so he could learn to hear what his wife was *really*
saying.

With the ears of an elephant to listen to God's voice speaking,
imagine what we might hear. In the spiritual life, listening to God is
essential. God commanded, "Hear, O Israel and be careful to obey "
(Deut. 6:3). To hear, we must learn to listen. Learning to listen to
God is an acquired skill. Often we only hear a lot of noise within our
souls. Between a noisy heart and a screaming world, listening to God
takes discipline. Yet God will enable his people to hear, because it's
his will that we listen for his voice.

Listening to God leads to a connected and satisfying life. God pleaded with the children of Israel through the prophet Isaiah, "Listen, listen to me, and eat what is good, and your soul will delight in the richest of fare. Give ear and come to me; hear me, that your soul may live" (Isa. 55:2b–3a). God's encouragement to listen will result in real life.

Samuel's story, told in 1 Samuel 3, offers insight into a young boy's soul. Samuel mistook the voice he heard in the night for that of his teacher and master, Eli. Finally Eli realized that Samuel was really hearing the voice of the Lord. Samuel's simple statement "Speak, LORD, for your servant is listening" (v. 9) is a prayer of invitation for God to speak. As Samuel, we may not be sure what we are hearing, but the more we listen, the better we distinguish God's distinct voice.

It's noteworthy that Eli helped Samuel discern what was going on. Friends can be tremendous assets when we share what we hear God saying. Sometimes we can hear the Lord speaking in the voice of friends or family. God also speaks in worship, perhaps through a song or the message. But the surest place to hear Him, where God primarily directs us to listen to Him, is in the Scriptures. The Bible offers the only direct revelation of God's heart. Hebrews 4:12 reminds us that "the word of God is living and active."

We can hear God in the still, small voice with which he spoke to Elijah. Elijah expected God to communicate to him in a dramatic way, but God chose to speak in a gentle whisper. Let the words of Clara H. Scott's 1895 hymn, "Open My Eyes that I May See," be your prayer:

> Open my ears, that I may hear
> Voices of truth Thou sendest clear;
> And while the wavenotes fall on my ear,
> Everything false will disappear.

*Your Soul Sense*

1. How have you heard God speak?
2. In what ways do you make time to listen for God to speak?
3. How can you learn to be "quick to listen" to others as in James 1:19? Would your life be different if you listened more?

# 53

# The Marvel of Touch

Oh, I have slipped the surly bonds of earth . . .
Put out my hand, and touched the face of God.

JOHN GILLESPIE MAGEE JR.

People were bringing little children to Jesus to have him
touch them, but the disciples rebuked them.

MARK 10:13

My dog Buster loves to be touched. On most mornings, he nuzzles his head into my hands so I can pet him. Most people have something in common with my dog. We need the touch of a human hand to be assured of love and acceptance. Babies who do not feel human touch will not thrive and may not even survive. Human beings were made with a need for touch.

This God-given and amazing sense helps us realize the presence of God, which is beyond the human touch. Through touch, we know that we are not alone. The simple touch of a hand upon your shoulder; the brush of a hand against your back in a crowded meeting; the stroke of a face with tender hands and the caress of a finger all awaken the assurance that we are alive and regarded by someone else. Through touch, we know that we are loved, wanted, and valued.

Hands laid upon a person's head traditionally have signified that the one who touches is imparting a special blessing of affection or empowerment. The laying on of hands is shown in the Bible when someone is sick. The touch of our hands symbolically transfers our hearts, hopes, and longings for blessing, healing, and hope.

Souls are shaped by many hands. Hands teach, coach, heal, give mercy, correct, and guide. The touch of hands of all types, colors, and sizes helps us expand in our soul.

Thomas was a disciple of Jesus who doubted the reality of the Resurrection when others gave the news to him. He wanted to touch the wounds inflicted on the cross before he would believe that Jesus was alive. Touch matters. One woman believed that she could be healed by merely touching Jesus' clothing (Matt. 9:20–22). She was right (see 14:35–36).

Jesus is our model for healing, healthy touch. By the touch of his hands, he conveyed healing power. Jesus used touch . . .

- to calm his disciples when they were afraid (Matt. 17:6–8);
- to bless children (Mark 10:13; Luke 18:15–16);
- to raise the dead (Luke 7:14–15); and
- to wash his disciples' feet (John 13:4–5).

Through touch, we communicate love, affection, devotion, appreciation, value, and acceptance. The soul longs to touch and be touched and to embrace and be embraced. When the prodigal son returns home, his father embraces him in full acceptance and love (Luke 15:20). Imagine if the Father had crossed his arms and not reached out to the returning son. Such rejection would have been devastating to the son.

The embrace of arms around shoulders, the tender touch of a shepherd who "gathers the lambs in his arms and carries them close to his heart" (Isa. 40:11), help us know God's acceptance, and his validation of us as the true and authentic children of God.

## *Your Soul Sense*

1. What does an appropriate touch communicate?
2. Even though you can't physically feel God's touch, what indicates that he is present?
3. In what ways do you need to experience God's touch?

# The Goodness of Taste

Soul food is our personal passport to the past. It is much more about heritage than it is about hominy.

SARAH BAN BREATHNACH

So whether you eat or drink or whatever you do, do it all for the glory of God.

1 CORINTHIANS 10:31

*S*ome amazing cooks attended the first church I served as pastor. These fantastic cooks prepared their best recipes for church dinners. Apple pies, chicken and dumplings, barbecued ribs, fluffy biscuits, and coconut cakes crowded the tables in our fellowship hall. Fellowship and food complemented one another.

Both the Jewish and Christian faiths associate food, feasts, and banquets with commemorating days of faith and celebration. Certain foods played an integral part in these remembrances. Even Jesus chose bread and wine to symbolize for his followers truths about his body and blood in the Last Supper. A compelling image that many of us share is that of gathering in heaven around a great feast.

A meal becomes something more when we share food and table. Meals together go beyond satisfying physical hunger. People who share time together around a table share lives and souls. We are more likely to speak of things that are important and personal. When I call a friend and ask, "Hey, can we have lunch this week?" I'm not calling to say, "I know that we will both be hungry by Thursday. Let's eat together so that we can get some food." The lunch occasion serves as a backdrop for renewing our friendship.

Research studies have established a link between shared meals and a strong family life. Just a simple meal around the family table with positive conversation and care is required. This ritual becomes sacred, more than the intake of food. We literally "take in" each other as we share our days, plans, or laughter.

In the South, some dishes are called "soul food." These vary from place to place and culture to culture, but the foods include macaroni with cheese, cornbread, pinto beans, and greens. These are considered delicacies because of the memories they elicit, not because of the calories or carbohydrates in them. For others, soul food—or comfort food—might include mashed potatoes and meatloaf because Mom fixed it every Thursday night. These foods nourish our souls as well as bodies.

When we "break bread" together, we don't always approach this table in strength and gratitude. Our brokenness, however, is one thing that brings us to the part of worship in which fellow believers share the bread and drink as Christ taught at the Last Supper. This observance goes by various names, but it always connects the broken bread with Christ's broken body and the drink with his life blood that he gave for his people. When we taste something, we usually consume it and transform it into ourselves—it becomes a part of us. It is a mystery, but it is so. Our hope is that this "holy communion" becomes part of us also. The bread and the cup are where we are welcomed to "taste and see that the LORD is good" (Ps. 34:8).

## *Your Soul Sense*

1. Were mealtimes positive or negative experiences in your childhood home?
2. What are some of your comfort foods? What memories do they elicit?
3. How does a meal become more than simply eating?

# 55

# The Scent of the Sacred

Smell is a potent wizard that transports us across thousands of miles and all the years we have lived.

HELEN KELLER

Perfume and incense bring joy to the heart.

PROVERBS 27:9

*L*iving in the West is an exciting adventure. One evening our dog went wild, barking. It was a different bark than I'd ever heard. Something was happening outside that our dog sensed with his nose. I went outside to see what was going on. We'd left our garage door open, and a huge black bear was feasting on the leftovers from a freshly overturned garbage can. The smell of leftover pizza had drawn the bear to our home, and our dog's keen sense of smell had alerted him to danger.

We live in a world of vivid smells. Scientists tell us that human beings can distinguish ten thousand different smells. A home where freshly baked cookies are being taken from the oven has a fragrance quite different from the odor in a crowded, hot gymnasium. Smells draw us in or put us off. Peppermint, coffee, bananas, garlic, cinnamon, and roses all have distinct smells. Even a person who is blindfolded knows the difference. If cold or the flu affects our sense of smell for days, we miss the smell of coffee brewing or a favorite bath soap.

Memories are sometimes associated with certain smells. Walking by a lilac tree helps you recall the memory when, as a child, you visited your grandparents' house, where you sat outside near their lilac tree. Mothers can recognize their own babies by smell. Animals seek safety if they smell odors associated with danger.

The sense of smell is not without mention in Scripture. Paul tells us "We are . . . the *aroma* of Christ" (2 Cor. 2:15, emphasis added). The fragrance of Jesus can, in fact, be distinctive. At a recent retreat I led, our meeting was already in progress when a woman in her sixties opened the door to our room, entered, and announced, "I smell Jesus in here!" Everyone in the room started laughing with tears. What she meant was that she was happy to be at the retreat and to sense the Lord's closeness. Her words became a sort of code phrase for the rest of the weekend. Those who tried to explain their personal encounter with the Lord on a walk or through Bible study would talk as if Jesus was so close they could tell by the aroma. Have you ever smelled Jesus?

Some church traditions use incense or scented candles in worship. While those from other traditions may see this as strange, the aromatic experience is meant to be a reminder of God's presence. In Revelation 5:8 we read of "golden bowls full of incense, which are the prayers of the saints." Incense was a reminder that prayers were lifted up to God like the billowing smoke rising to the heavens. Remember that the infant Jesus received certain gifts, including highly valued aromatic spices (Matt. 2:11).

We have noticed before about the enjoyment Jesus must have received when Mary anointed him with expensive perfume. "The house was filled with the fragrance of the perfume" (John 12:3). The smell that filled the air was confusing to some, but Jesus affirmed Mary's intent of worship and love, the real aroma of her act. He told her that people would speak of it for years to come—and we do.

When people who love God come together, there can be a sweetness to that particular time or event that will make you sense the presence of Jesus. Paul reminds us that we give off "the fragrance of life" (2 Cor. 2:16). We recognize in each other that strange, mysterious sense that we have been with Jesus, a spiritual fragrance.

The Bible often attaches importance to fragrance, incense, and smells. When one of our other senses wanes, another sense often compensates. Helen Keller, blind and deaf, enjoyed an acute sense of smell. This particular sense can become sharper and stronger, able to discern and keenly be aware of danger or alarm.

At the conclusion of one worship service at a church we visited, some friends and I were noticing how the order of worship was so arranged that worship leaders did not call any attention to themselves. They had seemed almost invisible. One of my friends was especially appreciative that "I did not smell any ego in that sanctuary. I really was able to worship the Lord."

### Your Soul Sense

1. Do you associate any smells with fond memories?
2. Do physical smells have any part, intended or unintended, where you worship? Is there a spiritual aroma to worship and fellowship?
3. What is one way you believe you have "smelled" Jesus?

# The Power of Imagination

It is not knowing a lot but grasping things intimately and
savoring them that fills and satisfies the soul.

IGNATIUS OF ANTIOCH

God is far higher than you can imagine, far deeper than
you can comprehend.

JOB 11:8 MSG

$S$piritual emaciation and stunted spiritual growth are serious issues facing people today. Such failure to thrive spiritually begins
with a mind and soul that cannot sense, cannot be moved, and cannot be humbled by God.

There is a skeptical fear among many today about being manipu-
lated by personalities and programs. Followers of Christ long to be
moved by God and sense the mystery of the presence of the divine.
We long for an encounter with the transcendent God but too often
settle for far less.

Soul care includes unleashing our God-given imagination. We
can imagine ourselves, for instance, living life with Jesus. Imagination allows modern-day followers to see themselves in the pages of
Scripture. When we read the stories of people within the inspired,
sacred pages, we need not remain on the sideline, a passive observer.
We can enter the stories of those people and make their stories our
stories. When Jesus offers the woman at the well living water, we see
Jesus offering the ladle up to our thirsty souls. We want to drink all
the water, taking it down to the parched parts of our souls that have
never been satisfied by anything or anyone else. When Jesus heals

the man who was lowered on the mat through the roof of the house, we see our friends carrying us to Jesus. Do we have such friends? When Jesus touches and loves the children, we imagine ourselves being invited to come and be close to Jesus and lean into him. His hand on our shoulder—that is the touch of life, is it not?

Our God-given imagination allows us to enter into the stories with Jesus to see ourselves as a companion with him. We can imagine ourselves walking the dusty roads with him. We can imagine the faces Jesus looked at and the withered hands he healed. We can wonder what it would have been like to be with him at the wedding feast or the party at Simon's house. Would we have reacted differently from the disciples who joined him? At Mary and Martha's home, would we have been helping Martha with the meal or sitting with Mary at Jesus' feet? How would we react? What would we do? How would we feel? These are the questions that mean that our soul is engaging with more than a printed copy of the Bible.

Through our imagination, we search for God "beyond the sacred page," in the words of Mary A. Lathbury's hymn, "Break Thou the Bread of Life." We can use every God-given sense to sense God's movement in our lives and world today.

The Bibles left sitting on our shelves, gathering dust, will not transform our hearts; nor will acquiring more and more information. If information could change a person's heart, surely Jesus would have applauded rather than rebuked the scribes and Pharisees, who were indeed serious students of the Law. The Pharisees had mastered intellectual learning. What they lacked was experiencing the living God. It is when we experience Jesus that our lives change.

Encounter, experience, engage in, and explore—these are the behaviors that help us meet Jesus in new and fresh ways.

## Your Soul Sense

1. What moves you, makes your heart swell, or stirs your soul?
2. How can you use your imagination to enter the biblical stories about Jesus?
3. How can you encounter, experience, engage, and explore Jesus Christ?

# PART 9

# SOUL THREATS

*Facing the Obstacles to Soul Growth*

# An Extreme Makeover

You never change things by fighting the existing reality.
To change something, build a new model that makes the
existing model obsolete.

R. BUCKMINSTER FULLER

What this means is that those who become Christians
become new persons. They are not the same anymore,
for the old life is gone. A new life has begun!

2 CORINTHIANS 5:17 NLT

*A*t this writing, what is called "reality TV" is quite popular in the United States and some other countries. In fact, in the U.S. the entertainment form seems to have taken over television. Some of the reality show offerings involve some sort of "extreme makeover," either the structure of a house or the look of a person. Since the point is to make the change as radical as possible, the producers make before-and-after scenes a highlight of each program. The sought-after response is for the audience (or those involved) to scream with surprise and delight. Sometimes the gasp is so big, I feel I'm being sucked into the television. It's pure drama to watch such extreme transformations happen right before one's eyes.

I'd like to sign up for one of those shows. I wonder what the experts could do with a body like mine. Could I finally have hair? Could they remove pounds and inches from my waist? What would I even want to look like?

The hope for change dominates more than media. Gyms, support groups, self-help books, and even some churches bill themselves as ways to change something about ourselves. But to be extremely made-over requires a transformation of more than the body. Our life needs more than cosmetic change brought about by multiple surgeries. We need deep soul change. We need the new life promised by Scripture (2 Cor. 5:17).

Recently, I sat with a couple who asked for help. There was no warm-up period. When I asked the husband why he had come, he explained, "The reason I'm here is for you to help me forget the past ten years of my life. I'm miserable. I want to forget the problems and the hurt I've been dealt." As his story unfolded, one thing became immediately clear: No change on the outside would help. This man needed deep change, a soul change.

How do extreme makeovers of the soul happen after we've struggled with the same problems for years? A broken marriage or relationship isn't instantly healed; a man with deep anger doesn't find a resolution to ingrained behavior in one worship service; a woman who struggles with an addiction often faces an uphill battle to regain years of life lost through poor choices.

Consider the biblical examples of men and women who followed Jesus. These ordinary people experienced a deep and authentic makeover. Although they didn't receive changed bodies on earth, they did experience the transformation of life itself: a revolutionized purpose; amended values; altered relationships; and revised views of God. No one was the same after following Jesus. Jesus had a way of altering everyone's life. He still does. The transformation of the soul, however, is not an instant one-, two-, or three-week process. It takes a lifetime to experience all the transformation we need. It doesn't happen by watching the clock and saying, "Hurry it up! I want my makeover now!"

Paul reminds us that transformation begins at our conversion to Christ and continues throughout our journey on earth. Paul says, "There has never been the slightest doubt in my mind that the God who started this great work in you would keep at it and bring it to a flourishing finish on the very day Christ Jesus appears" (Phil. 1:6 MSG). What started at conversion continues until we reach heaven.

*Your Soul Threats*

1. What would you like to change about yourself?
2. How can you adjust your expectations about wanting immediate change?
3. When have you experienced lasting change? What transforming principles did you follow?[1]

# Soulful Addictions

It is hard to understand addiction unless you've experienced it.

KEN HENSLEY

I decide to do good, but I don't really do it; I decide not to do bad, but then I do it anyway. My decisions, such as they are, don't result in actions. Something has gone wrong deep within me and gets the better of me every time.

ROMANS 7:19–20 MSG

*P*eter's wife caught him staring mindlessly into the computer screen late one night. It was a repeated pattern of behavior, but it was even more than that: Peter's addiction to Internet pornography was destroying their marriage and eroding his soul into a full-fledged crisis.

An addiction promises to gratify the soul but never really satisfies. Addictions to drugs, alcohol, sex, shopping, pornography, or manic living promise to deliver something good. But in the end, we discover that our soul is not satisfied by substitutes for what God intended. When we're tethered to drugs, alcohol, food, adrenaline, or any thing or substance, we're not experiencing the freedom that God desires for us.

We can get medicated, numbed, high, buzzed, or whatever we seek from addictive behaviors, but in the end, an addicted person is a confused soul, not a healthy one. The addicted person loses the ability to tell reality from fantasy, and the person becomes confused about what really does satisfy.

Being hooked in the soul means allowing something or someone to control us. We're like a fish that's taken the lure and is truly caught. The unsuspecting fish bites down on what it thinks is a tasty tidbit, only to discover that, after having bit only once, it is hooked. At first the fish fights for freedom. It thrashes, tugs, and pulls, letting the fisherman know that it wants to remain free. But sooner or later, the fish gives up the fight, accepting the inevitable. This is what happens to an addicted soul. First there's the bite and then the hook.

How does the soul become unhooked? How does a person who has bitten hard get off the hook? The tremendous growth of support groups, Alcoholics Anonymous, and other addiction recovery groups offer insight. You don't get unhooked alone. Understanding, empathy, and acceptance are crucial weapons. Deep inside, the recovering addict joins other individuals, and a strong bond is forged to aid in recovery. A church in the twenty-first century that is involved in reaching the needs of people will seek to offer biblically based support groups to people who struggle with various issues and addictions. This beautiful ministry is soul care at the deepest level.

A friend of mine is finally dealing with his addiction to Internet pornography. After his first session at a clandestine sexual addiction meeting (since he was afraid he would be recognized), he called me on the way home and said, "Steve, you won't believe it. This was like being in the best church service I've ever been to in my life. I've never seen such love." He had found his belonging for recovery and more. He had found people who know the sting of the hook and what is involved in getting the hook removed.

Being unhooked from an addiction is being able to reclaim your life, the life you were meant to live. We can thank God that being set free by Jesus is not limited to the sins of lying, cheating, and stealing. Jesus' promise of freedom to the captives also is a promise to those imprisoned by addictions. That promise is meant for everyone, even those who have not been free of the hook for a long, long time.

## Your Soul Threats

1. When you look back at your family's history, what patterns of addiction do you see in parents, brothers, sisters, grandparents, aunts, and uncles?
2. What surfaces within you as you consider the possibility that you are hooked?
3. How can you be a friend to someone who is hooked on something?

# Confessions of a Workaholic

> If we always do what we've always done, we'll always get
> what we've always got and nothing changes . . . nothing
> changes.
>
> ALCOHOLICS ANONYMOUS

> I've tried everything and nothing helps. I'm at the end of
> my rope. Is there no one who can do anything for me?
> Isn't that the real question?
>
> The answer, thank God, is that Jesus Christ can and
> does.
>
> ROMANS 7:24–25 MSG

Admitting difficult truths about oneself can be liberating. When truth is flushed out, you find that there is no real reason to cover up. The problem with my addiction is that it's applauded by our culture and affirmed by the church. How unbelievably seductive it is to be locked into a sin that is affirmed by most people. This gives my addiction added power to hold me and others in its grip. It's been a slow death for me and countless others who are numbed by praise for our efforts and accomplishments. There is a mistaken belief that the motives behind all the effort are pure.

I'm a workaholic. There. I said it. This long-held vice is not new to me. In my travels I am continually reminded that my tribe is increasing steadily. An immense number of men and women run perpetually on a spinning wheel like hamsters, every day of every year. Like an alcoholic, I can smell someone like me a mile away.

Workaholism resembles a wild rafting trip. I love the noise and swirl of whitewater. Activities, possibilities, and unrealized potential intoxicates. When it comes to work, the slow adrenaline rush I enjoyed from doing my work no longer was enough. I needed more feeling of being needed and important. Because I was reasonably gifted, people gave lots of reward to reinforce my addictive behavior. A vicious cycle began: The harder I worked, the more I was told I was valued and important. Living only for the applause of people will result in getting stuck in nothing but whitewater.

I learned to live out a slow death. If I had been hooked on drugs, alcohol, or pornography, maybe I could have gotten help sooner. There are support groups for these addictions. In all the churches and places I've visited, though, I've never seen an announcement that a group to help people like me meets on Tuesday nights at 6:00 P.M. in room 202. People like me get awards, not help.

The seductive roots of my sin extend back into my formative years. The era in which I was raised seems to have promoted workaholism. Ours wasn't the only family in which hard work was passionately modeled. I began my journey toward a living hell early, and in due course my sin spilled over into relationships with my wife and children. It left a sticky residue that we deal with yet today. I still have tendencies. I still work too hard, even in a ministry devoted to people who need to slow down to experience soul care.

Freedom did not come quickly. I had to learn or relearn basic understandings about life, love, and God. Despite advanced degrees in education, I needed to take remedial study for the course Jesus 101. Most important, I had to be reminded about what the gospel really means. It was a slow, arduous journey. I'm still recovering. I sometimes hear voices in the night that call out to me, "Do something impressive. Do something significant and you will finally BE somebody." These are the roars of sea monsters that must be slain each day, and I walk with a limp through this area of spiritual growth.

When Jesus was called "the beloved" of God (Matt. 3:17 NLT), he could no longer hide his divinity in a quiet undistinguished life. Immediately he had to launch himself on a trajectory of high visibility. In his human nature, Jesus had complete confidence that he was the beloved, so he moved confidently, passionately and sacrificially offering God's love.

Knowing who we truly are is an important step in our recovery from any sin that has entangled us. Each of us apart from our own merits or accomplishments is the beloved of God. No matter how hard we work or what else we achieve, we can earn no higher praise or approval.

## Your Soul Threats

1. What enticements to workaholism do you see in your national culture?
2. In what ways are workaholics applauded and affirmed? Why?
3. How can you tell if your work life is in balance and not headed toward addictive behavior?

# Sins of the Soul

Physician of my sin-sick soul,
To thee I bring my case;
My raging malady control,
And heal me by thy grace.

JOHN NEWTON

He who covers his sins will not prosper,
But whoever confesses and forsakes them will have
    mercy.

PROVERBS 28:13 NKJV

*S*in. Perhaps we'd rather not talk about it. You start sounding religious right away when that word enters the conversation. In 1973, psychiatrist Karl Menninger wrote a critique of culture that asked the provocative question, Whatever Became of Sin?[1] We can try to downplay sin, ignore it, suppress it, deny it, or refute it. The fact is, there is a soulful reality called sin. Even our own conscience affirms that reality.

Then again, the Bible makes it very clear that no one escapes the grip of sin. There's no camouflaging that sins of the soul wreak havoc in our relationships with God and one another. We have seen that, left unchecked, the soul "implodes," robbing us of new life. Sin is still the greatest threat to the soul. Even in our culture, where discussions about sin are couched in user-friendly terms, sin remains the threat. In both Hebrew and Greek, some of the terms relating to sin have to do with "missing the mark." Sin is like an arrow that misses the target. Sin means we've all missed the target altogether. Try as we might to deal with sin ourselves, it rages on.

There is no soul care until we deal with the issue of guilt for our sin. Often we treat the symptoms of sin as we would treat symptoms of the common cold. We take a cold tablet to stop our noses from dripping, but that doesn't cure the cold. God provides the only cure for sin-sick souls in the incarnation, life, death, and resurrection of Jesus Christ, the Son of God. Only God could deliver us from sin's grip through Jesus Christ.

*Savior* is a beautiful word. The assurance of being "saved" from sin by a loving Savior is the greatest blessing extended to Christians. Jesus opened his ministry by telling people to repent (Mark 1:15). He called men and women to turn and change direction. This is what *repent* means. Jesus calls us to leave sin and to embrace the good news. Sin made us head in one direction. Now Jesus calls us to turn away from that dead end. When we turn around and change direction, our sin-sick souls find the healing we need.

Why should we be embarrassed to use the bold words that Jesus used when speaking of sin? Sin is a threat to our souls, and Jesus knew that quite well. That's why we call him our Savior.

## Your Soul Threats

1. How does sin rob you of soul care?
2. If we are to care for our souls, how do we need to deal with sin?
3. How can confession affect the soul?

# 61

# Soul and Body

Our bodies have now become the Bethlehem of Jesus.
Jesus lives in us and takes up residence within.

OSWALD CHAMBERS

Didn't you realize that your body is a sacred place, the
place of the Holy Spirit?

1 CORINTHIANS 6:19 MSG

Some religions teach that the body is the enemy of the soul. Their beliefs insist that the body is evil and only the soul is good. In fact, some followers of these religions treat their bodies harshly in an attempt to elevate their souls.

As Christians, we know that our bodies help us to pray, serve, connect with others, and express our faith in practical ways. We consist of both body and soul, and caring for one means caring for the other. Soul care and body care go together. The incarnation of Jesus celebrated the human body. When God became flesh (John 1:14), he validated the human body as human flesh revealed his glory. Jesus' body served as a vehicle for spiritual living.

Our souls are not free-floating spirits. Our souls reside in physical vessels that are wonderfully designed and made of muscles, bone, and skin (Ps. 139:14). The soul dwells in what Eugene Peterson calls "a sacred place," interpreting Paul's use of the word *temple*. When we embrace our bodies as sacred places, we are motivated to care for them properly. We are better servants when we care for our bodies. Yet how often are we tempted to do things that harm our bodies:

- Burning the candle at both ends when God has told us that the body requires rest. We are to devote one day out of seven to restoring the body and soul.
- Eating improperly when God has told us to practice moderation. Remember Daniel's self control. Instead of the king's rich foods and dainties, Daniel preferred a simple diet. It preserved his health and spiritual gift of discerning dreams (Dan. 1).
- Remaining in addictions such as compulsive eating, abusing prescription drugs, or smoking. Victory over such addictions occurs only as the person admits defeat and surrenders to God.
- Ignoring simple hygienic practices that prevent diseases, such as flossing, frequent hand washing, and drinking clean water because we're usually on the run.
- Underexercising when a walk through God's nature tones the body and refreshes the mind.

Others are focused on their bodies, but they don't believe in the existence of the soul, or they ignore its reality. These individuals may take exercise to manic excess, undergo repeated plastic surgeries simply to postpone aging, or take dangerous hormones to increase physique or athletic performance. Such obsessions indicate a failure to believe that humans are made in God's image.

It seems that a healthy soul-body connection lies somewhere between neglect and obsession. Without our bodies, we cannot do anything on this earth. And, because the body houses the soul, the body matters to God. Soul care, then, includes care of the body, and it all adds up to self care.

## Your Soul Threats

1. How can you balance the needs of your body and soul?
2. How can you better practice self care?
3. What barriers might you erect toward self care?

# 62

## Soul Carnage

Often, in order to stay alive, we have to "unmake a living" in order to get back to living the life we wanted for ourselves.

DAVID WHYTE

If we confess our sins, he is faithful and just and will forgive us our sins and purify us from all unrighteousness.

1 JOHN 1:9

*A* man I know worked excessive hours for years with an insatiable appetite to succeed at almost any cost. He had, indeed, paid the price to get to the top. It was beginning to dawn on him, however, that the view from the top wasn't what he'd expected. After achieving his professional goals and fulfilling what he'd always seen as the reason for his being, he crashed.

He was appalled to realize that the lives of his wife and children were in ruins. His wife announced that their marriage was over. In the absence of love from their father, his teenage children were searching for love and intimacy in cheap substitutes. After spending his life at work, he had no real life. He was a junkyard in which trophies were piled and the deeper, more important things abandoned. This frightened man was alone and for the first time honestly assessed the carnage. The injuries were deep and extensive.

Spoiling some of the most beautiful scenery through our countryside are car junkyards. These automobile graveyards provide a final resting place for the twisted remains of long-abandoned vehicles. Through the years, the bright paint, shiny chrome, and clean interiors were degraded into shadows of their lost beauty. What was once wonderful has now become a forgotten heap of ruin.

We all have this junkyard carnage in our lives. For some, the journey has been so steep, arduous, and intense that when we ponder our inner landscapes, we see only the destroyed remnants. No man or woman navigates the potholes and bumps without carnage. For some of us, the wreckage accumulates quickly; for others, the heap gathers slowly and with little warning. Each personal junkyard has its own accumulation of unfulfilled dreams, regrets, and broken vows. In each the challenging question is the same: "What will I do with all of this junk? Is anything salvageable? Can any hope be restored?"

Zacchaeus would say that it can. He was a hated man who amassed a fortune by pressuring people to give more money in taxes. Included in his junkyard of carnage was the undeniable reality that he had cheated, abused relationships, and betrayed his own people as an agent for the Romans. Yet Jesus saw the value of Zacchaeus. Jesus restored value to the junk and transformed the carnage. As a result of Jesus' visit, Zacchaeus knew joy such as he had never before known. Meeting Jesus changed everything for Zacchaeus. Inviting Jesus to clean our souls changes everything.

Jesus seeks out people like Zacchaeus. He goes to where carnage has amassed and hope has been lost. After His encounter with Zacchaeus, Jesus gave us an amazing insight into his mission. He tells us, "The Son of Man came to seek and to save what was lost" (Luke 19:10). If you feel lost in the carnage of your own soul, do what Zacchaeus did. Invite Jesus inside, and let him restore all that is lost.

### Your Soul Threats

1. Where is the carnage in your soul?
2. What do you see in surveying the scene of your junkyard?
3. How could meeting Jesus in your junkyard inspire you to change?

# Satan and the Soul

I do not fear Satan half so much as I fear those who fear him.

TERESA OF AVILA

None of this fazes us because Jesus loves us. I'm absolutely convinced that nothing—nothing living or dead, angelic or demonic, today or tomorrow, high or low, thinkable or unthinkable—absolutely nothing can get between us and God's love because of the way that Jesus our Master has embraced us.

ROMANS 8:37–39 MSG

*O*ur family has been among many generations to sing a children's song. Actually, the song is an American slave spiritual that has appeared in many versions over the last couple of centuries:

> This little light of mine; I'm going to let it shine.
> This little light of mine, I'm going to let it shine.
> This little light of mine, I'm going to let it shine.
> Let it shine! Let it shine! Let it shine!

Our children especially enjoyed this song because they got to act out motions accompanying the words. Index finger candles were high in the air, waving furiously. The faster the candles were waved, the more the fun. One of the verses was about not letting Satan take our light away:

> Won't let Satan blow it out.
> I'm going to let it shine.

One could even leave out the word "blow" and do the action instead, almost as if we were sending the Devil to the side where he belonged.

Even for adults who know that Satan isn't so easily handled, it is important to understand that Satan may be more powerful than us, but he is nothing next to God. An essential belief of all Christians is that there is one God, not two. This single belief lies at the foundation of our worldview and our claim to believe what the Bible teaches. I know people, though, who live as if Satan is on the same level as our God, whatever they confess. The universe is not constructed around a dualistic power structure, with half of the power belonging to God and the other half to Satan, with people caught between them in an interdivinity tug-of-war.

The Bible makes it clear that an Evil One exists. He is referred to by several descriptive names. One of the most expressive is *Satan*, meaning "accuser; adversary." He is someone who condemns and opposes. During his time on earth, Jesus had to face the power of Satan to delude and tempt and even inhabit the lives of people. Jesus did not question that Satan ruled world systems and governments (Matt. 4:8–10 and parallels). But Jesus never ascribed to Satan any actual power. God alone is all powerful and rules history according to his plan. Jesus would have wholeheartedly joined the generations of Jews who daily repeated Deuteronomy 6:4–5, "Hear, O Israel: The LORD our God, the LORD is one. Love the LORD your God with all your heart and with all your soul and with all your strength."

Satan is active and alive in our world today. As adversary, his aim is clear. He is a liar, schemer, and thief who "prowls around like a roaring lion looking for someone to devour"(1 Peter 5:8). We need to be alert. We need to be aware of his crafty ways of bringing us down and his attempts to obscure the Christian's identity in Christ as God's beloved. The roaring lion stands defeated with the power of sin through the work of Jesus Christ. Satan can only tell lies to and about us. He can heckle, but his role in the game is limited.

Yes, we should watch out, but we should also watch for our Savior and Deliverer from Satan's accusations. Jesus Christ knows what Satan can and cannot do. Jesus was the sole victor in the wilderness and on the cross. The glorious loosening of the cords of death in Jesus' tomb defeated Satan. That Jesus rose from the dead is proof that he has power over Satan. Every time we celebrate Easter's proclamation that "the Lord is risen," we affirm God's reign in the universe. The light of Jesus will not be blown out by the Evil One, nor will ours.

## Your Soul Threats

1. If you are a new creature in Christ, how do you still experience Satan's opposition?
2. How do you stand against his schemes (see Eph. 6)?
3. When he encountered Satan, Jesus used Scripture. What Scripture verses can you use to help you stand against the Devil's schemes?

PART 10

# SOUL SEARCHING

*Finding Comfort in Difficult Times*

# 64

# SALVE for the Soul

The lesson of wisdom is, be not dismayed by soul-trouble.

CHARLES HADDON SPURGEON

Dear brothers and sisters, whenever trouble comes your way, let it be an opportunity for joy. For when your faith is tested, your endurance has a chance to grow. So let it grow, for when your endurance is fully developed, you will be strong in character and ready for anything.

JAMES 1:2–4 NLT

*I*t was said of the farm in E. B. White's beautiful children's story, *Charlotte's Web*, that "every day was a happy day and every night was peaceful."[1] This setting for a story in children's fiction, though, doesn't describe real life very well.

We collect soul wounds, nicks, and bruises along the journey of life. No one is exempt from hurt and trouble. People say hurtful things. Friends can disappoint. Rejection leads to a hemorrhaging heart. There's simply no shortage of possible hurts along the way. Pain is inevitable, and no one can escape being mauled by it.

So how does the soul heal? How can we find solace in trouble? When we scrape a leg or arm, we can apply ointments and lotions that promote healing. But is there healing ointment for a wounded soul? There is a SALVE for the soul that we can offer one another when trouble and hurt arrive. *SALVE* is an acrostic that helps us remember how to soothe a soul. By applying SALVE, we foster hope for the journey and healing in our souls. Safety, Acceptance,

Listening, Vulnerability, and Exploration each say something about how God uses us to ease pain and trouble:

- *Safety.* If the wounded soul is to heal, it needs a safe place and a safe person. A safe person listens without judging or giving advice. Silence and acceptance grows safety between people. The safer a hurting person feels, the more of the wound that can be revealed. Healthy communities and families that value safe places will resist the temptation to "fix" the situation. I came home from work one day to find my wife, Gwen, on the couch, crying. Someone had said something that hurt her deeply. Gwen said, "Steve, I don't need you to fix this. I just need you to sit with me and listen." Often, just being heard without feeling judged, taught, or fixed, helps the most. I wanted to "fix" Gwen's hurt, but I couldn't. I'm thankful that I was able simply to "be there" for Gwen.
- *Acceptance.* When hurting people share what they are feeling, acceptance is vital. A person who doesn't feel accepted will retreat back into the wounded self. Acceptance invites the hurting person to emerge and explore what has been held in private. In *Why Am I Afraid to Tell You Who I Am?* John Powell writes that we are afraid to tell people who we really are because people may not like who we are, and who we are is all we've got.[2] Acceptance means loving the hurting with unconditional love. It is lavish grace offered in the face of ugly sin. Whether the sin is done to or by the hurting person, that person needs the love that Jesus offers. While not accepting the sin, Jesus offered grace to the woman caught in sin. He simply said, "Neither do I condemn you" (John 8:11).
- *Listening.* A safe friend grows those elephant ears mentioned above to listen when the hurting soul needs to talk or process something. The person who seeks to provide safety listens from the heart, entering into the pain. Read 1 Corinthians 13, where Paul describes love. Paul's words offer a beautiful picture of a person who listens well. The listening ear is long-suffering and

patient. Often, it simply takes time for the hurting person to get something out on the table. A patient ear reflects a loving heart.

- *Vulnerability.* Often those who can provide SALVE have themselves been wounded. The hurting person senses a personal story in the listener that makes them feel safe. A listener who shares a true personal story helps the hurting person connect. A hurting person can sniff out the fake.

- *Exploration.* Underneath the Old Faithful geyser in Yellowstone National Park, underground canals and reservoirs hold the water that erupts on a precise schedule. Geologists exploring these vast reservoirs found an amazing system of natural underground piping.[3] A hurt person requires the same kind of exploration. The first thing the hurting person mentions may not be the true source of pain. But exploring the first issue can often lead to a deeper source. Perhaps the situation that is first mentioned is just the latest in a long series of hurts. By exploring the wound in grace and with truth, the listener often finds a deeper reservoir of pain.

Applying the SALVE in Jesus' name, we offer soothing words to restore the soul.

## Your Soul Searching

1. Who in your life has applied SALVE when you most needed it?
2. Which SALVE qualities seem important as you help in the healing of a hurting friend?
3. How does Jesus apply SALVE to your hurts? Through what people?

# 65

# Marred Souls

My fear for you is not failure . . . but of success in things
that do not matter.

HOWARD HENDRICKS

Whenever the pot the potter was working on turned out
badly, as sometimes happens when you are working with
clay, the potter would simply start over and use the same
clay to make another pot.

JEREMIAH 18:4 MSG

*H*ORSE is a simple game of taking turns shooting at a basketball
hoop. Someone makes a shot. Everyone else has to make the shot
from the same place. The first time you miss a shot, you get the letter
"H." The second time you miss you get an "O." Spell out HORSE,
and you're out.

The tension rises as letters accumulate. You hope for better shots,
but if you miss too many, you lose. When our family plays, we added
the "mercy shot rule" to give an extra chance to someone who has
gotten all of the letters. Without the mercy shot, there's no hope of
remaining in the game.

Mercy shots would be nice to have in the game of life. On that
court, failures, fractures, and fissures can be costly. After mistakes
or poor choices a person can feel that life is essentially a loss. From
a failed test to a wrecked marriage, mistakes and bad decisions can
leave a thick, sticky residue on the soul. Will the remorse ever end?

Beth felt this way after her divorce. She limped along with a deep
sense of guilt, as if the fracture in her soul disqualified her from a

fulfilling life. Through many conversations and in God's grace, she came to sense that God could use this experience to help others endure similar trauma after a marriage breakup.

Jeremiah illustrates the marred soul by describing a potter working clay into a pot on the wheel (see Jer. 18:1–6). At first, the soft clay seems to be forming into something useful. Then something goes wrong. An unexpected blemish causes the pot to wobble. As the wheel keeps spinning, the form that was nearly complete collapses.

A marred soul also carries such imperfection. What once looked good now seems spoiled. In factories where clothing, china, or other materials are made, marred products are called rejects. They are disqualified and separated from the perfect objects. But does marred clay or a collapsed soul need to be rejected? No, hope lies in the skill of the Potter. He returns the blemished clay into a lump and begins again, making something different.

Sometimes events or decisions turn out badly. The unexpected and unplanned happen. Failure and sin enter our lives uninvited and unwanted. Yet we're not cast away when failure mars the clay. No mistake is so big that it can't be reworked by the Potter, who knows what to do. The blemished soul can be reclaimed and reformed—transformed, actually—into something totally different of great value.

The miracle is that the same clay is used. There is no refuse, nor is the failed clay discarded. The blemish, the fractures, the failures become part of the transformed pot.

## Your Soul Searching

1. What is marred in your life?
2. How can you allow the Potter to reshape this?
3. How is the Potter reclaiming your marred clay?

# Disappointed Souls

If we will be quiet and ready enough, we shall find compensation in every disappointment.

HENRY DAVID THOREAU

In you [God] they trusted and were not disappointed.

PSALM 22:5

My son aspired to replace Michael Jordan as the twenty-first-century basketball icon. But he was cut from his high-school team. Along with this rejection came a sense of deep disappointment. He had always played basketball with zeal. His parents thought he just might have the moves, the skill, the touch, and the ball-handling finesse to provide many nights of games, yelling, cheering, and celebrating. When he got cut, our souls also were pierced.

At first, we were shocked. It made no sense. There must have been a mistake. Our son must not have heard the coach correctly. I secretly plotted my strategy: I would call the coach and set him straight. I'd share my disbelief and astonishment. Then the coach would admit that he had, indeed, made a mistake. The coach would tell me that my son could play, and all would be well. Of course none of that happened. I never called. I'm thankful that I didn't.

Who wants to drink from the cup of disappointment? There's nothing but bitterness in that cup. Yet disappointment is something every human soul drinks—a broken engagement, the long-hoped-for job awarded to another, the dream house sold to someone else, a mammogram that comes back showing a suspicious lump. Each time I do not get what I long for, disappointment floods my soul. But we have to handle the disappointment when love fails or children make horrendous choices, or we've made a big mistake in our job, so we tell ourselves to "suck it up," and we go on. Should we suppress the feelings of rejection since there are so many of them?

Jesus didn't. I don't think we often consider the tremendous disappointments that Jesus experienced. He faced rejection and disappointment unlike anything in our lives. His response marks a pathway to self-understanding, so that we do not thrash around in angry soul agitation.

Jesus was "a man of sorrows, and familiar with suffering" (Isa. 53:3). He knew enough sorrow to earn the title Isaiah gave him. He had sorrows and occasions of disappointment. People rejected him. Leaders scorned him. Jesus navigated through each disappointment as it surfaced. He never became sour and angry or bitter. Disappointments shaped his human nature, adding humility and compassion even for those who rejected him. Jesus forged a life of steel through disappointments and grief, so he was able to meet his ultimate goal.

Since my son came home with the devastating news of his rejection from the basketball team, we've had conversations that we never would have enjoyed had he made the team. Yes, that's a very big price to pay, but these talks have been important milestones for us to stand on and to connect as men, as father and son. It's been good for both of us to taste disappointment together and to survive.

## Your Soul Searching

1. What disappointment stirs your soul now?
2. How can Christ's example help with this disappointment?
3. How can God heal the disappointments of your soul?

# The Stressed Soul

Sometimes the most important thing in a whole day is
the rest we take between two deep breaths.

ETTY HILLESUM

But in their distress they turned to the LORD, the God of
Israel, and sought him, and he was found by them.

2 CHRONICLES 15:4

*Y*ears ago our young family started a church in Europe. It was an
amazing if challenging opportunity. Despite the blessings, it was
a stressful time. The beginning days of our struggling congregation
were touch and go. Life seemed fragile. Everything we worked and
prayed for could easily fall apart.

One evening Gwen and I sat in bed, talking about all of our
stresses. Suddenly, we heard strange noises. They were coming from
inside of me. My stomach was making loud groans. During the next
night, the same thing happened, and Gwen encouraged me to go to
the doctor. His diagnosis: stress. "Steve, your internal organs are not
happy. They're stressed out by the tension in your world," the doctor
explained. I had internalized all of the church's problems, and my
stomach was turning flips as I tried to find solutions.

Stress builds inside for a variety of reasons. Daily hassles of work,
traffic, and appliance breakdowns can push us toward the edge.
Good and bad life events can do it, such as the birth of a baby, a new
job, a move to a new city, or the death of a loved one. Today's world is
filled with stressful threats of human-caused and natural disasters.
Dis-ease make it hard to cope.

Still, stress isn't unique to our time and culture. Consider these calls to God from a stressed-out psalmist:

> Give me relief from my distress;
>     be merciful to me and hear my prayer (4:1).

> In my distress I called to the LORD;
>     I cried to my God for help (18:6).

> Look upon my affliction and my distress (25:18).

> Be merciful to me, O LORD, for I am in distress (31:9).

David wanted relief from distress. In fact, this is a theme through-out the book of Psalms (see, for example, 34:4; 55:17; 69:29; 72:12; 107:6; 120:1). Distress is the anxiety or mental suffering that accompanies stress. This soulful suffering produces a strain. Over time, this kind of stress leads to burnout and exhaustion. Prolonged stress can result in physical illnesses.

Discovering how to cope with stress is important in the care of the soul. Coping is beneficial for the stressed person and for those with whom the person lives. Practicing self care can make a huge differ-ence for family and friends. Here are simple suggestions for dealing with stress:

- Pray. David prayed about his distress and asked God to help. Prayer addresses what makes us feel distress. Talking things out with God keeps us from keeping them inside.
- Keep a sense of humor. Laughing about what you can't control is one way to relieve stress. A friend of mine likes to watch the old film series *The Little Rascals*. He laughs all the way through the shows. The Bible reminds us, "A cheerful disposition is good for your health; gloom and doom leave you bone-tired" (Prov. 17:22 MSG).
- Exercise. Regular and consistent care for the body lowers blood

pressure and reduces stress. Walking is one of the best forms of exercise.
- Sleep. When we feel bone-tired, we are also soul-tired. Sleep is God's way of replenishing the soul. Psalm 127:2 says, "In vain you rise early and stay up late, toiling for food to eat—for he grants sleep to those he loves."
- Stay close to friends. Healthy friends who create safe places for you to share your stress help to lessen the load. Scripture tells us to "carry each other's burdens" (Gal. 6:2).

De-stressing allows the soul to relax and to be more open to what God desires. It's important to find and regularly practice the right stress-busters.

## Your Soul Searching

1. What are three things that cause stress in your life?
2. How do you express your stress to God?
3. What is one thing you can begin doing to reduce stress?

# The Anatomy
# of Discouragement

Discouragement is simply the despair of wounded self-love.

FRANÇOIS FÉNELON

What can you do when the spirit is crushed?

PROVERBS 18:14 MSG

*A* few friends prayed for me during a season of discouragement. In trust, I wrote a candid e-mail expressing my need and requesting prayer. Some of the responses were surprising. One friend said, "Steve, thank you for confessing and articulating how I feel nearly every day of my life." This honest response was jarring, especially that he lived constantly with these awful feelings.

Discouragement is not new to the people of God. Abraham, Moses, Ruth, David, Jonah, Jeremiah, Peter, and Paul all experienced discouragement. We're in good company when we feel as if the wind has gone out of our sails. It doesn't mean that we've done something wrong. It means something is missing inside.

The word *discourage* is from the Middle English words *corage,* meaning "heart," and *des,* meaning "deprived or taken out." We become discouraged when the heart is taken out of us. It's a powerful image because being discouraged is just that—having no heart to face the present or the future. Being discouraged means that we don't have "it" in us to keep going. We want to quit. We want to sit down. We want to surrender.

Sometimes friends try to help us when we feel discouraged. They give us solutions and suggestions to help us regain what we've lost.

But often their words can seem empty and hollow. Sometimes no human words, hugs, or rewards can replace the holes in our chests. We realize our hearts are simply not engaged anymore. We try to be encouraged, but for whatever reason the glass still looks half empty. We've walked in sadness for so long, we don't know how to get out.

It's helpful to read the psalms of David. They are a window into David's soul, showing that this man with a heart for God, often lost heart. David tells about his feelings of despair and vulnerability in Psalm 42:

> Why am I discouraged?
>> Why so sad?
> I will put my hope in God!
>> I will praise him again—
>> my Savior and my God!
> Now I am deeply discouraged,
>> but I will remember your kindness.
>>> Psalm 42:5–6 nlt

Read this entire psalm and see if you can understand his loss of heart. David's words are riveting and brutally honest. He doesn't hold back or hide his feelings from God. He asks straightforward questions.

When we read David's words, we have confidence that God can handle our feelings. We don't have to hide how we feel. David poured out his soul, and so can we. Asking the hard questions of God sometimes helps us understand, even if God doesn't remove the trauma. God can take the truth. He knows the way we feel. There's no need to hide it.

## Your Soul Searching

1. When you feel discouraged, to whom do you normally turn?
2. What happens to you and your life when you feel discouraged?
3. Can you write a psalm or a paragraph to God, expressing your feelings?

# The Aroma of Failure

A man who fails well is greater than one who succeeds
badly.

THOMAS MERTON

I'm on the edge of losing it—
   the pain in my gut keeps burning.
I'm ready to tell my story of failure,
I'm no longer smug in my sin.

PSALM 38:17–18 MSG

*F*eelings of failure have a way of introducing us to three unwanted
traveling companions: Shame, Blame, and Guilt. These familiar
adversaries often show up in my life. I can hide, but somehow it's
inevitable that they find me.

When feelings of failure take the form of shame, blame, and guilt,
we end up wading in the quagmire of disappointment. They nip
at the heels and heckle with dark and depressing voices that success will never happen. In my case, they will not let me forget that
I've failed at something. Shame, blame, and guilt speak their mind.
Their voices taunt, "You are a disappointment. You'll never reach
your goal. You've failed too much already."

How do we rid ourselves of these unwanted travel mates? It's been
said that when someone begins living as a Christian, self-rejection
and self-condemnation are among the last of the old ways to die.
Somehow we are able to resurrect these old voices from deep within
us. So we need to listen to God's voice when he speaks about our
identity as his beloved. He extends acceptance. God's voice does not

condemn. Christ's death on the cross assures us of this. What happened on the cross will not fail us now or at any time in the future. We are covered by God's great outpouring of love. His shouts of love can drown out the jeering voices of shame, blame, and guilt.

Learning to listen to the other messengers of God's love is also important. I have a friend who often asks me, "How much have you been listening to your old companions this week?" It's a great question—one that I need to ask many times.

How about you? Do these feelings come to you when you fail at a job, relationship, task, assignment, or goal? Can you hear the voices when you fail and break a commitment to never do something again?

## Your Soul Searching

1. What unwanted companions travel with you?
2. How does God's voice remind you of who you really are?
3. In Zephaniah 3:17, how does God quiet the accusing voices?

# When You Feel Broadsided

There's a divinity that shapes our ends,
Rough-hew them how we will.

WILLIAM SHAKESPEARE

You were jarred into turning things around. You let the distress bring you to God, not drive you from him. The result was all gain, no loss.

2 CORINTHIANS 7:9 MSG

*O*ften there just are no words in the English language to express some of our deepest feelings. Gwen was born to missionary parents and raised in Ethiopia. Ethiopians speak a language called Amharic. It is a difficult language for Westerners to comprehend. There are 250 characters in the Amharic language, while English has only 26. Many of the sounds of this language are explosive and guttural, while others are soft. Gwen uses an Amharic expression when nothing in English expresses the emotion.

When Gwen was diagnosed with breast cancer a few months after her mother died from cancer, only the Amharic term, *gragruban*, seemed to fit the shock and distress. *Gragruban* means, "some unexpected thing has entered from the left. I don't understand it." Her diagnosis was a blow that had come from the left.

When something hits unexpectedly and leaves us feeling ambushed and breathless, as if the wind were knocked out, this is the feeling of *gragruban*. It is the result of uninvited trauma. If we could see what was coming, we could prepare. But when something enters from the left, we are left shocked and searching for meaning.

The word I use is *broadsided*. I read last week that a family of three traveling in Colorado were broadsided by another vehicle. The family was out on an errand, then in a moment the parents were dead, and the small child who had been strapped into his infant car seat was an orphan. Many experiences cause a person to feel "broadsided." Life offers little insulation from such experiences.

Paul reminds us that "we must go through many hardships to enter the kingdom of God" (Acts 14:22). The older we grow, the more we realize the fragile nature of our lives. One phone call or e-mail can change everything. Learning to endure hardships is a great challenge. Pain pierces the soul of those who, minutes before, had been living cozy lives. Enduring this kind of pain helps us dig through the "fluff" of life to find real meaning, purpose, and strength.

Initially those who sustain sudden *gragruban*, or feel that they have been broadsided, feel helpless and struck down. Strength beyond ourselves is required to move on through. When Paul was broadsided, he confessed, "The Lord stood at my side and gave me strength" (2 Tim. 4:17a).

Only the presence of Christ can give the strength to stand firm.

## Your Soul Searching

1. When have you felt broadsided?
2. How did you feel toward God during this time?
3. How do you find God's comfort in the midst of trauma?

# The Furnace of Transformation

Every morning I must say again to myself—
today I start.

ANTHONY OF THE DESERT

He knows the way that I take;
when he has tested me, I will come forth as gold.

JOB 23:10

Clay is shaped, molded, and formed in the making of pottery, but the process isn't complete until the clay is fired. The heat of the firing process hardens the shape and makes the form strong, durable, and usable. We like another kind of fire—one that warms but doesn't burn. The glow of the fire, the blazing red embers, and the invitation to "sit and be warmed" is far different from fiery furnace transformation, but only deep, penetrating fire generates transformation.

Everyone faces the fire that shatters or transforms. Ask anyone who's entered that furnace through a divorce, a lost job, or the grief of losing something else that was considered precious. People who have endured a furnace of transformation attest that there's nothing else like it. The fires can become so hot and furious that the one tested wonders whether survival is possible.

Several years ago my wife and I entered a furnace of transformation. A long-awaited dream had come true. We were thrilled. But it soon began to crumble. The fires of transformation heated up quickly. We found ourselves among the casualties of a devastating implosion. We had no income, and our future seemed suddenly fragile. We thought our world had ended. Our world as we had known it did end, but we emerged from that fiery furnace with more than we realized. Although we'd lost much, we survived with our naked souls transformed. The furnace changed the way we looked at trials, at God, and at our own hearts.

We now barely recognize that previous life because so much has changed within and without. Fire does that to a person. Once you feel the singe of the fire you begin to give up expectations. You bend low into the process and trust the hands of the One who brought you there. The fire of transformation removes a person's options. Choices are few, and the answers are simple. You simply have to endure the process.

The potter's furnace is where true transformation occurs. Without the heat, and without change the pot will not last. The heat of the furnace causes a melting, galvanizing, and bonding. Soft clay becomes a useful product. Without the fire, there is only softness to admire. Fire has a way of removing the superficial and making us appreciate what is eternal. We emerge with durability, resolve, faith, and, yes, appreciation.

Fire also is required to refine crude ore. The prophet Malachi tells us that the Lord "will sit as a refiner and a purifier of silver; He will purify the sons of Levi, and purge them as gold and silver, that they may offer to the LORD an offering in righteousness" (Mal. 3:3 NKJV). As fire hardens clay, it separates impurities from precious metal. This is what God desires for us: a transformed soul, purity of heart, and a singleness of purpose for his glory.

## Your Soul Searching

1. What furnace have you been in lately?
2. What does this feel like?
3. How can you benefit from the furnace fire without being destroyed?

# 72

# Cocooning Toward Change

"I'm making a cocoon," said the caterpillar. "It looks like I'm hiding, I know, but a cocoon is no escape. It's an in-between house where the change takes place. . . . During the change, it will seem . . . that nothing is happening, but the butterfly is already becoming. It just takes time."

TRINA PAULUS

Wait for the LORD;
be strong and take heart
and wait for the LORD.

PSALM 27:14

Waiting isn't easy; we don't like it. The microwave doesn't work fast enough; the computer modem is too slow; change takes too long. Children can't wait to grow up. Our culture is obsessed with pragmatism, and it's just not practical to wait.

Things were different when Jesus walked the planet. He walked everywhere. These slow journeys gave the time for many life-changing conversations.

Jesus did a lot of waiting, too. He waited about thirty years before he even began his revolutionary public ministry. From our North American perspective, we wonder what Jesus could have accomplished if he had started earlier and had longer to minister.

But Jesus waited. He waited in the wilderness. He waited in the garden. He waited for his own execution. He waited in the tomb. Jesus learned the rhythm of waiting. We must learn the same rhythm if we are to grow, change, and become like Jesus. Although it seems inefficient, waiting is a necessary step toward spiritual maturity. Waiting cannot be bypassed, as much as we might wish that it could. We cannot become like Jesus overnight.

Something transformational happens when a person learns to wait. The caterpillar spinning its cocoon is not preparing a place of escape but a place to wait for transformation, a sanctuary for change. The time of waiting is actually a season of becoming. In the dark, the caterpillar waits for the moment of rebirth, when it emerges transformed, re-formed, and very different.

Transformation doesn't come if we move too quickly. We need to make space for God. When we wait and are still, God comes near (Ps. 46:10). The place of waiting can provide asylum, not to hide but to hear God. Jonah heard God only in the cocoon of a fish's belly.

Waiting, then, invites us to change, and change requires endurance. The invitation to change ushers in a different kind of living. During the cocoon time, transformation is spun around us, and there's nothing to do but let the waiting do its sacred work. If we wait, we change.

Moses *waited* in a cocoon of wilderness for forty years. Paul *lingered* in Arabia for three years after his dramatic encounter with Jesus. Jesus *remained* in the tomb for three days. Something happens in the cocoon that can happen nowhere else. As we grow, pressure builds inside and the room to move dwindles. Change happens. Transformation begins.

Waiting sets aside the unimportant and allows the one waiting to be seized by the eternally significant. Through waiting, we find that our wings to soar are more than wings of butterflies. We are taught to soar on wings like eagles (Isa. 40:31).

## Your Soul Searching

1. What are you waiting for?
2. Why is it difficult to wait?
3. How can you thrive during this waiting time?

# PART 11

# SOUL COMPANIONS

*Friendship on the Journey*

## 73

# The Meaning of Companionship

Without spiritual companionship I shrivel and die inside.
Above all, I need a spiritual friend or group of friends of
the soul who are able to see right through me and love
me as I am.

ALAN JONES

Am I my brother's keeper?

GENESIS 4:9

Nine miners were trapped in a coal mine in Somerset, Pennsylvania. The breaking news left millions of people around the world deeply concerned. For days, those nine men were imprisoned hundreds of feet beneath the surface of the earth. It was the worst-case scenario. In the course of enduring nearly eighty hours of darkness, the miners took action and huddled together.

Later they recounted how they tied themselves together with ropes and huddled back-to-back, keeping body contact to stay warm as cold waters flooded their air pocket. They were determined to live or die together. One newspaper called this story, "A Miner Miracle."

The power of unity enables survival when the cave-ins threaten. When things that formerly seemed solid are collapsing and the world falls apart, we need to be tied to others. Would anyone dig me out of life's rubble? Who would lay down their life to save me? Would I lay down my life for another? Is something more important than survival?

The miners encouraged one another through times of despair.

They were stalwart companions. One of the miners said, "Everybody had strong moments. . . . At any certain time, maybe one guy got down, and then the rest pulled together, and then that guy would get back up, and maybe somebody else would feel a little weaker. But it was a team effort. That's the only way it could've been."[1]

The word *companion* originates from a French word that combines the words translated "with" and "bread." The word paints a picture of two beggars searching for bread together. Companions search for something together, not alone. The miners' soulful companionship helped them survive entrapment and the threat of death.

God's people are shown being strengthened by companionship in the biblical accounts of their lives. Ruth and Naomi faced their plight together. David and Jonathan and the disciples of Jesus were strengthened through unity.

Companionship is a life-giving necessity. The miner miracle in Pennsylvania calls us to think through our mutual commitments in life and work. We need companions to help us grow in the midst of life. Do you have that kind of unity with anyone?

## Your Soul Companions

1. What does companionship mean to you?
2. Do you have a close companion? If so, who?
3. Have you experienced companionship with the Lord Jesus Christ?

## 74

# The Heart of Companionship

Every deed and every relationship is surrounded by an atmosphere of silence. Friendship needs no words—it is solitude delivered from the anguish of loneliness.

DAG HAMMARSKJOLD

The LORD God said, "It is not good for the man to be alone. I will make a helper suitable for him."

GENESIS 2:18

*A* few years ago our family relocated to a new city. Early every morning I watched my school-age boys bravely march out to catch the bus loaded with kids and head for their new school. We all hoped that they soon would have friends. Being new *and* a teenager combines for a particularly deep angst. But no person is immune to loneliness.

There doesn't seem to be enough *withness* in life. Withness is the soulful dynamic of walking through life in tandem. It is the soul's heart cry that, truly, it *is not* good for us to be alone. Jesus offered withness to his companions. The account of Jesus' ministry in Mark reports that "He climbed a mountain and invited those he wanted *with him*. They climbed together. . . . *The plan was that they would be with him*" (Mark 3:13–14 MSG, emphasis added).

Jesus offered his companionship, calling others into a life with him that was greater than life alone could be. The withness that Jesus offered is something to consider because he offers the same companionship to us.

Life alone? Never in Jesus' way of living. We need times alone to think, evaluate, and talk with God. But this is not life alone. Rugged individualism and self-sufficiency run counter to the biblical concept of companionship. These states of aloneness are our own defenses to shield ourselves from being rejected and wounded. Our souls thirst for intimacy, but sometimes we refuse to fill the cup and drink, too suspicious of deep companionship.

Life without relationship is contrary to the nature of a God who exists in community as Father, Son, and Spirit. Companionship is in the very nature of a God who created humans to live together. So how does withness work in a high-rise office building in a large city? How does it work for someone who is single and cut off from hope of marriage? We see the theory, sense the need, and still feel alone.

To experience the power and depth of a lingering conversation at lunch, or on a drive or walk, is soul medicine. That's because companionship is of God. We may have to wait for his provision. We should, of course, take initiative in seeking relationships of various kinds, but we can't force soul companionship. Jesus didn't. Soul companionship is a process of building through shared experiences, testing, and trials. Jesus forged connection with his disciples over three years, and then he felt their rejection and betrayal. But the dance of companionship has an allure that beckons even the wounded to join in.

Companionship is a grace gift to hold sacred. Once you find a companion, keep guard over that relationship. Companionship is something we should pray and hope for.

## Your Soul Companions

1. What is the difference between being alone and being lonely?
2. Who are the best companions you have known?
3. Do you feel stuck in loneliness? What can move you toward others?

# 75

# The Lost Art of
# Having a Buddy

Friendship doubles our joy and divides our grief.
Swedish proverb

Agree with each other, love each other, be deep-spirited
friends.
Philippians 2:2b msg

*A* buddy of mine ordered grits for breakfast. Paul was from the
North and had never enjoyed such a delicacy. He asked the waitress, "Can you please tell me what a grit is?" I smiled quietly on the
outside but was roaring with laughter on the inside as the waitress
chuckled and said, "Honey, there's no such thing as a grit. Grits come
in community."

People, like grits, are best in community, not in isolation. John
Donne said the same thing about people when he penned the
powerful words, "No man is an island, entire of itself."[1] Consider
these facts from the *Wall Street Journal*:

- In a study of 2,800 men and women over age sixty-five, those
  who had more friends had fewer health problems, and they
  recovered faster.
- Researchers at Yale University surveyed death rates among
  10,000 older adults with different degrees of social contacts.
  They concluded that having friends reduced the risk of death
  by half over their five-year study.
- In another study of the health of 6,800 adults in Alameda

County, California, it was determined that, among older adults, friendship played a more important role in longevity than did having a living spouse.[2]

Yet the art of having a "buddy" seems to be less common today. Having a close friend is life giving, yet our culture devalues interpersonal commitments of all kinds and especially friendship. E-mail and the Internet have contributed to this disconnection. E-mails—however frequent and newsy—are not the same as a lingering conversation and a deep interpersonal connection.

Part of the problem is that we have become oriented to round-the-clock production. We develop routines and connections around what needs to be done: work, chauffeuring, going to meetings, setting appointments, making investments, using the cell phone for down-to-business conversations, and cramming more stuff, more information, and more news into life. Who has time for friends?

It's hard for people to be spontaneous with others. Recently, we tried to find a night when we could socialize with two other couples. It took three months to find a date that worked for everyone. Another friend was planning a fortieth birthday bash and sent out invitations a month ahead of time. The party had to be rescheduled because there were too many time conflicts. An event that happens once in a lifetime was moved to accommodate everyone's busyness. We really need to examine that level of life frenzy. The lost art of "buddyship" needs to resurface in our lives or we're headed for some shipwrecks.

Human beings were created to live in connection, not isolation. More than fifty times in the New Testament, Scripture addresses how we are to relate with some form of the words meaning "one another." The Bible calls God's people to pray for, love, encourage, accept, teach, and serve one another. Christians are to bear one another's burdens. These "one another" passages are more plentiful than instruction to evangelize. Spirituality exists within community. Evidently, God saw this as a basic human need and made sure that we had lots of reinforcement in the Bible about friendship and community. Something spiritual happens when we are together.

Jesus said, "When two or three of you are together because of me, you can be sure that I'll be there" (Matt. 18:20 MSG)

So friendship is a mandate, even if it requires us to swim against the current. And because friendship is a gift of God, it's worth the effort to have a real buddy. It is part of soul care to be a friend and enjoy friendship.

## Your Soul Companions

1. What are some barriers to friendship in your life?
2. What defines a "buddy" in your experience?
3. What should we do if we are without a buddy?

# A Soulful Advocate

There is nothing on this earth more to be prized than true friendship.

THOMAS AQUINAS

Two are better than one, because they have a good return for their work: If one falls down, his friend can help him up. But pity the man who falls and has no one to help him up! Also, if two lie down together, they will keep warm. But how can one keep warm alone? Though one may be overpowered, two can defend themselves. A cord of three strands is not quickly broken.

ECCLESIASTES 4:9–12

My sister has become a grandmother for the first time. I've watched her come alive in this new role. She wants to be "the best grandmother ever." It's become her mission. She lavishes love on this granddaughter, speaking into her soul such endearing Southern words as "Pumpkin Pie," "Baby Doll Face," and "Sweeter than Sugar."

When they spend time together, my sister focuses attention solely on her granddaughter. They take long walks. She reads storybooks that this tiny child cannot possibly understand. She touches, holds, and caresses this little soul with lavish love. She sees this little girl as truly "grand," a tender soul who simply needs to be loved.

Oh, that each of us had someone to see us that way. Everyone longs to be fully recognized and accepted for who they really are. Many people know that they need to have such a soulful advocate, a person who is "souly" for them. An advocate literally is "one called for another." We cannot do life alone, nor were we intended for the aloneness that permeates our culture.

Eugene Peterson, author of *The Message*, offers insight into the role of a soulful advocate.

> Each of us has contact with hundreds of people who never look beyond our surface appearance. We have dealings with hundreds of people who the moment they set eyes on us begin calculating what use we can be to them, what they can get out of us. We meet hundreds of people who take one look at us, make a snap judgment, and then slot us into a category so that they won't have to deal with us as persons. They treat us as something less than we are; and if we're in constant association with them, we become less. And then someone enters into our life who isn't looking for someone to use, is leisurely enough to find out what's really going on in us, is secure enough not to exploit our weaknesses or attack our strengths, recognizes our inner life and understands the difficulty of living out our inner convictions, confirms what is deepest within us. A friend.[1]

A soulful advocate is this type of person. Beyond our performance, abilities, gifts, and aspirations, a soulful advocate lets us "be." My sister delights in the essence of who this new *grand*-daughter is. Surely, the child knows and senses this, for it is innate in us to recognize love. This ability is the mark of infinite and divine love upon us.

This distinguishing, unconditional love is powerful, transforming, and safe. This is the love of God, our most holy soulful advocate.

## Your Soul Companions

1. What people have been your soulful advocates?
2. Who do you want to be a soulful advocate for you now?
3. What are the characteristics of your soulful advocate?

# 77

# About Intimacy

Friendship is born at the moment when one man says to
another, "What! You too? I thought that no one but myself . . ."

C. S. LEWIS

I have called you friends.

JOHN 15:15B

Intimacy is a mark that we, as human beings, bear the DNA of
God. Intimacy is the God-given ability for two or more people to
be their true selves, feel comfortable in their own skins with each
other, and freely exchange all that makes us, and marks us as, human. The Christian faith expresses the intimacy experienced by God
in the biblical understanding of what we call the Trinity. The Father,
Son, and Spirit coexist in an intimate relationship. Since we bear the
image of God, we long to connect with others in safe, life-giving, and
mutually beneficial ways.

I am truly intimate with someone else when I let that person see
who I am, who I am not, and who I long to be. I am not intimate
when I am self-protective, guarded, and inauthentic.

My marriage and growing friendship with my wife has been a
long process toward this kind of intimacy. Every inch of progress
in this area represents gaining new ground for us to stand upon together. Cultivating new ground of closeness and intimacy isn't easy.
At times it seems we've been hoeing on opposite sides of the field. At
other times we've weathered gale-force storms. But we've also sheltered in arbors of sweet gladness together. Intimacy is not a given in
any relationship. It's fostered and grown like a well-tended garden
that in the end yields its own delicious fruit.

Creating safe places to be intimate is the real challenge. Can I trust you enough to tell you what I'm feeling? Will you value my heart if I expose it to you? Can past hurts and disappointments be healed enough for me to dismantle barriers of self-protection? What models can show me pathways to intimacy?

Intimacy seldom just happens. In my twenty-five-year marriage and my pursuit of friends, intimacy takes time, patience, failure, and forgiveness. There have been seasons of dormant intimacy and fantastic times of intertwining and healthy belonging.

Intimacy allows other persons to simply be themselves. It releases them from expectations, needs, and desires. It foregoes our need to have friends be exactly the way we want them to be. Becoming intimate is seeing one another as we truly are, holding no joy or envy deep within. Soulful intimacy grows over time as trust, safety, and experiences develop. Seeing the soul, caring for the soul, and loving the soul of another person is a remarkable privilege that should always motivate us to tread lightly and lovingly because we walk on holy ground.

It feels safe to grow in intimacy when we feel accepted, not judged; valued, not discounted; celebrated, not ignored. Feeling safe with a friend is knowing that all we really have is who we are. If we feel rejected or discounted, then we simply will not allow another person to get close enough to see into us.

When we relax in each other's presence with no pretense—no agenda other than simply to be with each other—intimacy flourishes. To know and be known is a deep cry of the human soul. This longing and desire moves us to risk coming close. The soul leaps within the person who connects in this deep way. There is joy within and a satisfaction that only an intimate friend can give.

## *Your Soul Companions*

1. What does intimacy mean to you?
2. What does it mean to feel safe with another person, truly to be yourself?
3. How would you describe your friendship with Jesus?

# Archiving and Forgiveness

> As long as we do not forgive those who have wounded
> us, we carry them with us or, worse, pull them as a heavy
> load.
>
> HENRI NOUWEN

> See to it that no one misses the grace of God and that no
> bitter root grows up to cause trouble and defile many.
>
> HEBREWS 12:15

*A* computer program occasionally displays a message, asking whether old files should be archived. When "yes" is indicated, files I haven't looked at in months are placed into a file called "Archives." They are still there—somewhere deep within the hard drive—ready to be opened as needed.

A computer archive is like a room filled with filing cabinets of musty old files. The soul also has an amazing ability to archive. It stores old hurts and wounds, disappointments and incidents that happened years ago. Those drawers of old files remain if anyone dares open them up. They're invisible, but we know that they're there. We say that we forgive someone who's hurt us, but deep inside that injury can be archived and stored until something triggers memories. Then, without warning, a drawer pops open, catching us off guard. We explode in anger. Something triggers a painful memory. We try to avoid someone we see on the street who we once knew.

So how can the soul deal with those contaminated archived files? The answer to archiving is forgiveness. When we forgive each other, we release the archived hurts to another file called "Deleted." We make the decision not to carry the wound, nursing it, and holding another person responsible for our pain.

Unless we forgive, we will accumulate contaminated files. Offering forgiveness to the one who hurt us blocks the ability to archive the hurt. When we give up the archived file, we find release from its dominion over us. We also liberate our souls from the role of offended party.[1] Hurt and an inner desire to "set the record straight" makes a heavy burden to carry through the years. True forgiveness says, "Delete that old, unresolved file. You don't need to carry it in the hard drive any longer."

When we're forgiven for the hurts we've caused others, we also receive forgiveness, the remedy for corruption and contamination. When we're forgiven, we free ourselves from being the offending one. Jesus tells us to operate in this simple way. *Forgive freely, and be freely forgiven.* It's the mark of a thriving soul.

## Your Soul Companions

1. What issues might you have archived that need to be reviewed?
2. With whom do you need to give up the right to be offended?
3. How does being forgiven help cleanse the soul?

# Souls in Community

Let him who cannot be alone beware of community. Let him who is not in community beware of being alone.

DIETRICH BONHOEFFER

This is the very best way to love. Put your life on the line for your friends.

JOHN 15:13 MSG

*I*nside each heart is a secret passion, the longing to be in a relationship characterized by acceptance, growth and a sense of belonging. We desire to love and be loved, to know and to be known, to touch and be touched, to give and to receive. God created us with the need to be relational creatures, and in community we offer love and friendship to one another. In community, we find ourselves. When we live alone all the time, we live in delusion, deceiving ourselves. But when we have friends who are truthful, honest, and loving, we find who we really are.

The need for community is deeply imprinted on our souls. As beings who are created in the image of God, we are created also with the desire for community. God is not, after all, alone in his being. He experiences community in the Trinity of the Father, Son, and Holy Spirit. Likewise, we are not to be alone in our existence. To be truly human is to be in community and in relationship with other people.

The New Testament supports the idea of community through the experience of the church, but the biblical teaching on the church needs reexamining in our culture. Rather than stately buildings, community needs to again become the most important purpose.

In another meditation, we looked at the "one another" texts of the New Testament in relation to friendship generally. It is important to note, though, that those texts were directly about relationships within the church. Here are more than fifty references to living together with one another:

1. "Be at peace with each other" (Mark 9:50).
2. "Wash one another's feet" (John 13:14).
3. "Love one another" (John 13:34).
4. "Love one another" (John 13:35).
5. "Love each other" (John 15:12).
6. "Love each other" (John 15:17).
7. "Be devoted to one another in brotherly love" (Rom. 12:10).
8. "Honor one another above yourselves" (Rom. 12:10).
9. "Live in harmony with one another" (Rom. 12:16).
10. "Love one another" (Rom. 13:8).
11. "Stop passing judgment on one another" (Rom. 14:13).
12. "Accept one another, then, just as Christ accepted you" (Rom. 15:7).
13. "Instruct one another" (Rom. 15:14).
14. "Greet one another with a holy kiss" (Rom. 16:16).
15. "When you come together to eat, wait for each other" (1 Cor. 11:33).
16. "Have equal concern for each other" (1 Cor. 12:25).
17. "Greet one another with a holy kiss" (1 Cor. 16:20).
18. "Serve one another in love" (Gal. 5:13).
19. "If you keep on biting and devouring each other . . . you will be destroyed by each other" (Gal. 5:15).
20. "Carry each other's burdens" (Gal. 6:2).
21. "Be patient, bearing with one another in love" (Eph. 4:2).
22. "Be kind and compassionate to one another" (Eph. 4:32).
23. "[Forgive] each other" (Eph. 4:32).

24. "Speak to one another with psalms, hymns and spiritual songs" (Eph. 5:19).
25. "Submit to one another out of reverence for Christ" (Eph. 5:21).
26. "In humility consider others better than yourselves" (Phil. 2:3).
27. "Do not lie to each other" (Col. 3:9).
28. "Bear with each other" (Col. 3:13).
29. "Forgive whatever grievances you may have against one another" (Col. 3:13).
30. "Teach . . . one another" (Col. 3:16).
31. "Admonish one another" (Col. 3:16).
32. "Make your love increase and overflow for each other" (1 Thess. 3:12).
33. "Love each other" (1 Thess. 4:9).
34. "Encourage each other" (1 Thess. 4:18).
35. "Encourage one another" (1 Thess. 5:11).
36. "Build each other up" (1 Thess. 5:11).
37. "Encourage one another daily" (Heb. 3:13).
38. "Spur one another on toward love and good deeds" (Heb. 10:24).
39. "Do not slander one another" (James 4:11).
40. "Don't grumble against each other" (James 5:9).
41. "Confess your sins to each other" (James 5:16).
42. "Pray for each other" (James 5:16).
43. "Love one another deeply, from the heart" (1 Peter 1:22).
44. "Live in harmony with one another" (1 Peter 3:8).
45. "Offer hospitality to one another without grumbling" (1 Peter 4:9).
46. "Each one should use whatever gift he has received to serve others" (1 Peter 4:10).
47. "Clothe yourselves with humility toward one another" (1 Peter 5:5).
48. "Love one another" (1 John 3:11).
49. "Love one another" (1 John 3:23).

50. "Love one another" (1 John 4:7).
51. "Love one another" (1 John 4:11).
52. "Love one another" (1 John 4:12).
53. "Love one another" (2 John 5).

Since so much is said about being with one another, it must be important enough to require attention and affirmation. Living out the "one anothers" is a noble goal of the Christian life, as well as a soul need for the journey.

## Your Soul Companions

1. What people come to mind as you read the "one anothers"?
2. Circle the "one anothers" that you feel you receive. Underline the ones you wish you practiced more faithfully.
3. How can you celebrate relationship with those in community with you?

# PART 12

# SOUL
# SIGNIFICANCE

*Finding Meaning and Looking Ahead*

# 80

# The Elusive Nature of Success

The most elusive key to satisfaction is not getting what
you want—it's wanting what you get.

TOM MORRIS

Till I die, I will not deny my integrity.

JOB 27:5B

Tom Morris, who writes about succeeding in the business world,
observed that "Success should never be confused with wealth and
power. Rather, success should be linked to excellence and fulfillment. Success is about who you are, not what you have. Successful
people work to discover their talents, to develop those talents, and
then to use those talents to benefit others as well as themselves."[1]

Models of success loom larger than real life and seem to be out of
reach. Many "successful" role models followed by the entertainment
media gild their lives with opulent excess. Their houses and toys
evoke envy. But rarely do we stop and ask what these people sacri-
ficed to get where they are. What was the cost in broken relationships
and crippling personal problems?

We don't see all that weight below the surface when we look at the
iceberg of success. The little bit of their lives that we do see makes us
envious. But we might not want to know what is going on under the
waterline of their lives.

What is success? How do we attain it? To create a personal working definition of success, consider these ideas:

- I am successful if I'm fulfilled in life, not if I have filled my life with stuff.
- I am successful if there is meaning to life, a reason to get out of bed and face the day.
- I am successful if I have character and integrity.
- I am successful if my own story fits the larger story that God has for me.
- I am successful if I am surrounded by people who are pursuing a biblical lifestyle with me.
- I am successful if I finish the race well.
- I am successful if my goal for the next twenty-four hours is to love God and others deeply.
- I am successful when I walk humbly with God.
- I am successful when I do not need validation of success from other people.
- I am successful if I hear "Well done!" when I enter eternity.

Your personal definition of success depends upon how you define success. Take a moment and define what it means to you.

## *Your Soul Significance*

1. What successful people do you admire? Why?
2. Are these people basing their lives on biblical values?
3. Looking at the above list, which criteria for true success do you relate to most? Why?

# 81

# Soul Care and Money

There are three conversions necessary: the conversion of the heart, mind, and the purse.

MARTIN LUTHER

So if you have not been trustworthy in handling worldly wealth, who will trust you with true riches?

LUKE 16:11

It's impossible to consider the care of our souls without discussing money. Jesus knew that money and possessions threaten the soul. He spoke more about money and possessions than he did about prayer, heaven, or hell. He knew that the soul can go bankrupt over financial preoccupation, stress, and concern.

The state of the soul relates directly to attitudes toward money. If our hearts are set on gaining more, our preoccupation will be, "Do I have enough?" "How much more can I get?" We continually strive for more. In contrast, if we're generous with money, it satisfies our souls. About financial giving, Paul said to the Corinthians, "You will be made rich in every way so that you can be generous on every occasion, and through us your generosity will result in thanksgiving to God" (2 Cor. 9:11).

Jesus spoke about money and possessions in the context of relationships. Money can be a barrier in relationships that matter both here and in eternity. We can indeed gain the whole world but lose our souls (Matt. 16:26). If we allow money to grip us, it can choke the spiritual life out of us. If our thirst always is for more, it will never be quenched.

Sometimes it is easier to talk about religion or sex than to really talk about money. Personal wealth remains a deeply private issue. Yet money holds a power as does nothing else, to the point where Jesus called it a rival god as he declared our need of redemption from the soul-throttling power of possessions (Luke 16:13).

If our souls are to thrive, we must learn to handle money in a way that does not thwart the inner person. Being generous and grateful helps. Learning to be generous is a discipline that leads to soulful contentment, but it requires a transformation of mind and heart (Matt. 6:19–21; Rom. 12:2). Gratitude flows from the soul that frees itself from clutching God's gifts. The posture of a soul who recognizes the origin of money differs from that of one who still wants more.

Learning to care for our souls requires a look at how we care for money. By looking away, we deny the power that money, as Jesus said, has over our souls. Courageously facing this question head-on helps us explore our soul's longings and find true success.

## Your Soul Significance

1. What place do you give money in your life?
2. How can your soul be converted from the love of money?
3. How can you become a generous soul?

# 82

# Who Defines You?

*And now Lord, with your help, I shall become myself.*

SØREN KIERKEGAARD

*God's love does not allow us to remain as we are. It is more than acceptance. It works and forms, it carves out the image which God has intended. This is a lifelong process and sometimes a painful one.*

WALTER TROBISCH

*B*aking cookies after shaping the dough with a cookie cutter, Gwen wanted all of the pieces that came out of the oven to look the same. That's what the recipe called for. When it comes to cookies, sameness is delicious, but thank God, you and I aren't made with a cookie-cutter form. Each of us is made in the image of God, reflecting individually his image and glory. We are image bearers of God in some respects, yet each person is unique.

The purpose of life is not to become like others. Rather, God's intention is for us to become our true selves. By honoring and valuing distinctive individual qualities, we offer honor and glory to God. One of our goals is to grow in self-awareness. Knowing God is linked to knowing the true self. These two areas of knowing are tandem paths on the journey.

The more I learn about God, the more aware I am of myself. Augustine of Hippo, prayed, "Grant, Lord, that I may know myself that I may know thee."[1] Over a thousand years later, the Protestant Reformation theologian John Calvin began his systematic theology, *Institutes of the Christian Religion*, by speaking of the twofold knowledge of God and self: "There is no deep knowing of God without a deep knowing of self and no deep knowing of self without a deep knowing of God."[2]

It takes a long time to learn that we are not defined by jobs or accomplishments. When we meet someone for the first time, we usually reveal our culture's preoccupation with "doing" by asking two defining questions: "What's your name?" and "What do you do?"

I hope each of us learns the truth about self. We try on clothes and masks of various identities, only to realize later that we feel most comfortable in our own skins. Christians should stop trying to please others who want to define, categorize, or label.

Walter Trobisch, the Swiss psychologist, reminds us that one of life's greatest lessons is to "learn to accept acceptance."[3] When we accept and love who we really are, we are on the way to loving ourselves. But what Jesus asked of us is hard work. It's hard to accept our uniqueness when we compare ourselves to the other cookies on the shelf.

Only a God like the One who really exists can create so much difference in size, shape, color, texture, and personality. If God accepts us, then we have to wrestle with the question, *Why is it so difficult to accept myself?*

## Your Soul Significance

1. What do you like about yourself?
2. What part of you gives great glory to God?
3. How can you accept yourself at this stage of life?

# Desires of the Soul

The strength of a man's virtue must not be measured by
his occasional efforts, but by his ordinary life.

BLAISE PASCAL

Delight yourself in the LORD
and he will give you the desires of your heart.

PSALM 37:4

*A* men's Bible study meets Tuesday mornings in a coffee shop
where delicious goodies are baked. Those aromas create a di-
lemma: Should I eat a freshly baked muffin? That cinnamon driz-
zled, blueberry muffin calls out to me, "Pick me up and eat me."
Of course, it is not the blueberry that has developed a voice box or
particularly wants to be digested. My own desires are putting words
into the muffin's mouth. But do I really want that muffin? Wouldn't
I really rather lose weight and enjoy good health? I have to explore
the desire when faced with a muffin choice like this.

Facing our desires helps us explore what we really want and what
really matters. As we examine the longings of our soul, we come face
to face with some core issues that define us. Our desires tell us about
our values and what really counts among those values. There was a
time when position, status, and power were intoxicating. I wanted
the life of importance that these afforded and set out on a manic
pursuit to "arrive." I was living out the temptations of Jesus.

Early in his ministry, Jesus walked alone in the desert. There, he
encountered the issues that so often confront those who are allowed
opportunities for success. In Matthew 4:1–11, Satan tempted Jesus

with the great worldly compulsions: to be self-focused ("turn the stones into bread"), to be impressive ("throw yourself down"), and to be controlling ("I will give you all these kingdoms"). Face to face with dark choices and confronted by Satan with opposing evil force, Jesus modeled the values with eternal significance: God above self; humility above being celebrated; and obedience over control. Jesus desired God's way, God's values, and God's perspective about what is truly important.

Choosing to be like Jesus means deciding to be different when faced with conflicting desires and temptations. The daily decision to live like Jesus is a matter needing deep desire. Exploring the deeper desires of the soul helps us connect with soul-passions and heart-longings. What we want matters in our soul care. Desiring God, wanting what God wants for us, and understanding our own desires are all important parts of our soul care.

## Your Soul Significance

1. What do you really want out of life?
2. How do your own desires compare to what Scripture says God desires?
3. What would it look like for you to delight in God?

# The Power of the Dash

All men die, few men really live.

SCRIPT LINE FOR WILLIAM WALLACE IN THE MOVIE *BRAVEHEART*

Now that I am old and gray,
   do not abandon me, O God.
Let me proclaim your power to this new generation,
   your mighty miracles to all who come after me.

PSALM 71:18 NLT

*A* man named Alfred had the rare opportunity to read his own obituary. Because of a mix-up, his hometown newspaper reported that he had died and published his obituary.

Alfred had made his fortune by inventing dynamite in 1867. While he gave much to others, his obituary blamed dynamite for the death and suffering of thousands of people and referred to him as a "merchant of death." Dismayed by such a portrayal of his life's work, he determined to improve his public image and leave a better legacy.

A century later, we associate Alfred Nobel with peace, knowledge, and scientific advancement, not destruction. His Nobel Prize is an award bestowed on world-changing leaders whose lives make a difference in science, other disciplines of academia, and politics. Mother Teresa, Theodore Roosevelt, and Martin Luther King Jr. have been recipients.

Nobel had an unusual opportunity for a second chance. Nobel (1833–1896) lived eight years of accomplishment longer than the newspaper originally reported.

In describing someone's life, we can list the person's years of birth and death. The span in between is reduced to a dash. What will the life of Stephen W. Smith mean before the second date is filled in: 1954–? The date of death remains blank. It will be added one day—this year or decades from now. So far the dash spans over five decades of life. I hope there are more years since I don't feel "done" yet. I have dreams yet to be fulfilled. I devote my days to a ministry vision that I believe God implanted in my soul. It is up to God whether I do those things or someone else does them after the year of death is filled in. Still, I wonder: What will yet happen during the course of those years? Will they have been spent wisely or squandered? A meaningful legacy is a dash well lived, a life in which we loved God and others well. This is what matters.

People who think about the sum of their accomplishments are wise. They accept the truth of mortality and live in reality, centered and purposeful. Within the limitations of that dash, it is never too late to make adjustments and live with passion and meaning.

What will your life encompass in eternal values?

## Your Soul Significance

1. Write down what you would like on your tombstone inscription.
2. If you knew you were going to die in the next few months, what would you change? How would you spend your time?
3. The Quakers have an expression: "Let your life speak." What does your life say to others about what is important?

# Leaving a Legacy of Faith

Something should remind us once more that the great
things in this universe are things that we never see.

MARTIN LUTHER KING JR.

When David had served God's purpose in his own generation, he fell asleep.

ACTS 13:36A

*I*t is often said that no hearse pulls a trailer to haul possessions to
the cemetery. When we die, our bodies are buried, but what we
leave behind on earth is called a legacy.

The fast-paced world does not give us much time to consider the
question of how you will be remembered, but to leave a legacy, we
cannot put off thinking about the inevitable. All of us will leave behind some mark.

History marked the moment when United States astronaut Neil
Armstrong took the first steps by a human on the moon's surface.
At the time, newspapers around the world quoted the U.S. National
Aeronautics and Space Administration (NASA) claim that, if left un-
disturbed, the footprints left behind by the Apollo astronauts will
remain for 10 million years. There is no atmosphere, no weather, and
no wind to alter the impression made by a handful of adventurous
men.

Just like those footprints, every one of us represents a legacy—
what we bequeath to those who follow. Most of us would rather that
our lives leave a legacy of worth, imprinting its recipients with true
faith and values. I believe that the greatest gift is a legacy of faith.

A simple epitaph of King David of Israel is tucked into a sermon of the apostle Paul at Perga. When David was a young shepherd, he killed the giant Goliath, and he went on to became the greatest king of Israel. He established a nation and national identity and wrote some of the most inspiring thoughts in the history of world literature. Then, over a thousand years after his death, Paul said of David's life and death, "When David had served God's purpose in his own generation, he fell asleep" (Acts 13:36). Throughout his life, David served God's purpose in spite of challenges, failures, and setbacks. Even after committing awful failures, his greatest desire was to serve and please God. What a legacy he left!

A legacy is a lasting product of what matters to you now. Are you choosing to leave a legacy of faith? How are you proceeding? How we will be remembered tomorrow often is determined by how people see us walking in our faith today. We build our lives, characters, and legacies by acts, choices, values, and attitudes. When parents do not leave a godly legacy of faith, families suffer. And that imprint can affect entire nations!

## Your Soul Significance

1. Do you have a passion and purpose? If so, what is it?
2. How are you defining your legacy?
3. What would you like your legacy of faith to be?

# Holes in the Soul

I cried every day when I was born and every day shows
me why.

<small>GEORGE HERBERT</small>

Teach us to number our days aright,
that we may gain a heart of wisdom.

<small>PSALM 90:12</small>

*E*very legacy has an origin. Ours began the day we were born. Some of us are fortunate enough to be living a legacy shaped by a godly heritage. Our own legacies were shaped somewhat by how we were raised, whether in faith, love, and security or dysfunction and pain that leaves a burden.

One man recently described his soul as he tried to come to grips with issues of his past. He felt maimed by things that had happened: "It's like there's a hole in my soul like the holes in a piece of Swiss cheese." He told me about all the things he didn't get when he was a child. All of this left him feeling there were holes in his soul that nothing could fill.

He recalled all of the disadvantages and hurts he'd experienced early in life. But as we talked more and asked for God's guidance, he began to realize that his painful childhood had actually helped him develop inner strengths. God had leveraged a painful past to give him incredible gifts. A difficult past can be shaped into something tremendous for God.

Many spiritual advantages accrue to those who have walked a difficult path in life. I heard Joni Eareckson Tada speak in an auditorium filled with teenagers. Joni suffered near total paralysis from a diving accident when she was a teenager. The accident left her with a broken body but an amazing soul. She said she would not trade her wheelchair for a healthy life during which she would miss out on all that she's learned about God. When she made that statement, its significance almost exploded in my heart. It was an amazing story of transformation that she shared with those teenagers.

That night I considered in a new way the holes in my soul and my emotional paralysis because of the past. God used Joni to teach that he is able to use past pain for his glory. God would use past difficulties, mistakes, and failures to shape my soul for his glory. This would all be part of the legacy this life could pass on to others.

No one leaves an unmarred legacy. Most legacies have an outer story and an inner one. The outer story is what you see or remember quickly when you think of a particular person. You might remember a person and say, "Oh, he was a great leader" or "She was an amazing teacher." But he was more than simply a leader, and her life was more than teaching. An inner story is part of the legacy. An inner story represents what is not seen but is very much felt.

It's from there, those deep and often dark places where no one can see, that our legacies are truly formed. When our private worlds inform our very public worlds, when our inner stories converge with our outer stories, then our true legacies can be defined.

I've experienced pain, and many mistakes in my journey thus far. And I'm not finished yet. But it's what I do with my past experiences *now* that will speak into the future.

### Your Soul Significance

1. Is there something negative in your life that God can leverage into a legacy?
2. How is God's faithfulness expressed through your past?
3. How is God causing your past and your future to converge?

PART 13

# SOUL
# CELEBRATIONS

*Marking the Events of the Soul*

# Soulful Celebrations

Celebrate what you want to see more of.

THOMAS J. PETERS

To everything there is a season, a time for every purpose
under heaven: . . . A time to break down, and a time to
build up; a time to weep, and a time to laugh; a time to
mourn, and a time to dance.

ECCLESIASTES 3:1, 3–4 NKJV

*I*magine Jesus attending a birthday party for one of his followers,
such as Peter or Mary Magdalene. Can you envision Jesus throw-
ing a graduation party for his followers after they completed their
rigorous training and discipleship program? It's not a far-fetched
idea when we consider that Jesus attended weddings, enjoyed dinner
parties, and observed Passover feasts.

Jesus was a Jew who regularly practiced the rituals and traditions
of his culture. He participated in the customs, knowing that festivals,
pilgrimages, and traditions were part of faith and life. Such times
gave Jesus and his friends occasions to come together, to celebrate,
and to leave their work obligations. Specific food, drink, and rituals
set the time and event apart from the ordinary.

We all need such times. Special occasions help mark one day or
time apart from others. We gather together to celebrate, remember,
pray, and bless.

When we step outside of our ordinary lives and join family, friends,
and community to rejoice and give thanks, we participate in soulful
celebrations. They are soulful in that they nurture the soul. What

might have been done privately and alone is shared in the circle of community. Our joys are multiplied as the family of faith affirms what God has done through a particular place, event, or person's life. In such celebrations a collective, unified voice of heartfelt joy is shared. Through such celebrations, we declare that no one should be forgotten in God's big family. Retirement, graduation, birthdays, anniversaries, promotions, births—such milestones make festive times to share the joy.

Soulful celebrations help interpret the more important, deeper meaning of life for the community, family, and friends. Our souls need the joy of laughter, good food, music, and dancing. In these ways the soul celebrates life.

Practicing soul care involves celebration, through which Christians share their common experience as sons and daughters of God. These deep and soulful times help us remember, reflect, and recognize the meaning of our lives. We *remember* a person and take note of his or her life; we *reflect* upon what the person means to us and what our lives would have been like if we had never met this person. We remember the place or event and *recognize* that specific places and events really do matter. A soulful celebration underscores and highlights what is happening, not only in our individual stories but in our bigger circles of family, friends, community, and even the world.

Without soulful celebrations, our lives and culture will grow more secularized. Without sacred traditions, we will lose perspective and buy the myth that making a living is all that matters. In doing so, many of us will make a living, but we will not have a life.

Celebrations and rituals tie us together. They bring distant relatives "home," and unconnected people together in community. From the simple mealtime—when the family gathers around one table—to more elaborate and festive occasions, various events mark the time and designate people, places, and events that should be celebrated, blessed, or eulogized.

## Your Soul Celebrations

1. What special occasions did your family share when you were a child? Were any particularly meaningful?
2. Do you have favorite times of year? What makes them special?
3. How can you creatively practice soulful celebrations with family and friends?

# The Blessing of the Soul

Blessed is the influence of one true, loving human soul on another.

GEORGE ELIOT

Tell Aaron and his sons, "This is how you are to bless the Israelites. Say to them:

'The LORD bless you
  and keep you;
the LORD make his face shine upon you
  and be gracious to you;
the LORD turn his face toward you
  and give you peace.'"

NUMBERS 6:23–26

At a church in the Anglican tradition, a blessing is regularly given as part of the worship services. After an Anglican service, I overheard a young girl of about seven years old ask her mother, "Mommy, will you please give me a blessing?" The mother stopped as they were leaving the service, leaned over, placed her hands on the daughter's shoulders, and said, "Oh, Hannah, you are such a special daughter. You are pretty, smart, and have a wonderful heart. I love you so much and know that God has a special future for you."

The daughter broke into a bright smile as they walked on. I felt I had witnessed something significant—the blessing of a young girl's soul. The mother spoke words of affirmation, distinction, and honor into the soul of her daughter.

There's no doubt why the daughter desired a blessing after hearing it bestowed by the priest on the congregation at the end of the liturgy. God made us with souls that need and long to be blessed. The Latin word for *blessing* is the ancestral root of the word *benediction,* and it literally means "speak good." A blessing happens when one person speaks good things into the soul of another. Theologian and writer on spiritual life Henri Nouwen reminds us, "To give someone a blessing is the most significant affirmation we can offer."[1] A blessing is powerful and necessary because the soul needs to be affirmed. God fashioned our souls to need words that encourage—that literally speak courage into the soul.

In Bible times, the blessing was passed from father to son, from woman to woman, and from friend to friend. By speaking a blessing into the life and soul of another person, we participate in an act of affirmation and validation. A blessing affirms people for who they truly are, speaking words of life into their souls by reminding them of their true identity as Christians. As the world seems eager to invalidate the true identity of sons and daughters of God, blessing affirms it.

The act of giving a blessing is simple. You speak truth about that person. You do it personally and you can even place your hand upon that person to signify the giving. To receive a blessing means something more challenging. You simply must receive. You don't earn it or warrant it. You are given a blessing because of who you are, not because of what you have done. This is the grace of the Christian life. In some traditions, when one receives a blessing, one turns the palms upward, assuming the posture of a beggar who is simply receiving the blessing as it is given.

The giving and receiving of a blessing is practiced more in some families, groups, communities, and churches than in others. But the need to bless and to be blessed is universally a human need. A blessing allows us to hear again who we are and to lift our countenance to face the road ahead.

*Your Soul Celebrations*

1. What is the significance of giving and receiving a blessing?
2. Who has blessed you? In what way? Who would you like to bless you?
3. Who do you need to bless? How will you bless that person?

# A Birthday for the Soul

Grow old along with me! The best is yet to be.

ROBERT BROWNING

Long before he laid down earth's foundations, he had us
in mind, had settled on us as the focus of his love, to be
made whole and holy by his love.

EPHESIANS 1:4 MSG

For many years, a friend has never missed sending a birthday greeting. We no longer live in the same town. For some time we haven't even lived in the same country. But space and geography doesn't matter to that sort of friendship. This friend always remembers my birthday with a card. Thus I know that in this friend's heart I am never forgotten. The whole family looks forward to this one card as an event. As my birthday approaches, the children ask, "Did it come yet?" "Did Dad get his favorite card?" The card usually arrives right on the day.

To be remembered—not ignored or taken for granted—is powerful. I wonder why that's true. Perhaps we carry around a secret suspicion that we don't matter, that no one will notice. Will our absence matter at a meeting? If we don't show up, will anyone even notice? Questions like these can surface in our minds. Consequently, the celebration of a person's birth reinforces the fact that he or she matters. A celebrated birthday can assuage a soul that feels neglected and even unwanted.

When they were young, my children eagerly planned their birthday parties every year. We would sit at the same round table for each of our four kids, celebrating them, lighting candles, and singing the song they know so very well. They have big smiles, and their countenances are alive, bright, and full of life when we practice this birthday ritual. They know that they matter. From an early age, each son sensed that the song, the candles, the cake, and the people focused love and respect on him. Each boy intuitively knows, beyond the words, that he is celebrated on this day.

I suppose the real reason I long to receive my friend's card is that I have a strong, secret longing to feel that I, too, am celebrated. For all the time we spent together years ago, for the talks, lunches, and the common interests we shared, it is comforting to think that this person is still reaching out to say, "You mattered then, and you still matter. Steve, I'm still celebrating you, your life, and all that you stood for and now stand for."

The card doesn't say all that, so I know I'm reading a lot between the lines, but some sense of affirmation is implied in the card, whatever it says. Maybe we don't get this message in a card on a birthday. It can come in a variety of ways—a call, a few words of thanks or praise, a note, a warm greeting, or a hug. These actions communicate that we're special.

When we receive these loving gestures from others, we can remember that we also matter to God. Jesus expressed his great love and affection for the people he encountered. He noticed the unnoticed. He paused and considered the long neglected. He touched the untouched. He communicated the dignity of people when he singled them out and interacted with them.

Jesus thus gave worth, value, and distinction to those he encountered. Birthday celebrations help us do the same in a small way. By remembering others' birthdays, we have the opportunity to tell them that they are worth celebrating, that we are celebrating with them.

## Your Soul Celebrations

1. Of all your birthdays, which one stands out in your memory? Why?
2. If you could plan the ideal birthday party for yourself, what would it be like?
3. Who celebrates you? Who should you celebrate?

# Soul Passage

The secret of life is enjoying the passage of time.
JAMES TAYLOR

And Jesus grew in wisdom and stature, and in favor with
God and men.

LUKE 2:52

When each of our four sons turned thirteen, there was a special celebration to mark the crossing of the son into manhood. It was a time for us to realize that we needed to let go of parenting our sons like children and embrace them as young men. We modeled this ritual and celebration after the Jewish *bar mitzvah*, a coming-of-age ceremony. A young man's *bar mitzvah* is a night of celebration and commissioning.

For the Smith version, we invited friends, explaining why this particular time was so important as a night to understand the meaning of being an adult. Guests arrived knowing some of what would happen. We told them what to expect, since such a celebration is not normally practiced in a Christian home. Old friends who had joined us for our other sons' celebrations knew the significance by the time our youngest reached age thirteen. They were eager to participate in what was to happen.

The ceremony started in a circle to receive the son as an honored guest. He sat among us as an equal and took his seat in the circle. He had spent time with these family members and friends as a child, but now he sat *with* them as a fellow adult. He became one of us. Circles symbolize a sense of belonging and connection. We wanted to usher our son into a circle of friends who would speak words into his soul about being a companion—no longer as a child but as a friend.

Each friend had prepared significant words to share. The reality of the day-to-day world of an adult is that many ripping, degrading, and cutting words are said to us. People often feel like victims in their own homes, in the workplace, in the marketplace. But on this night, our son heard significant, positive, and kind words that warmly welcomed his soul into adulthood. We spoke of his qualities, the unique DNA he bears, the attributes he possesses that remind us of God, his heavenly Father. On this night, we affirmed our son's belovedness, calling him into manhood and speaking blessings about his worth and place in this world. We did this because we hoped he would never forget.

Each invited guest brought a gift that symbolized deeper truths of life. Gifts have included a compass (symbolizing direction), a magnifying glass (symbolizing curiosity), and a framed poem or Scripture verse of special significance. All of our sons have collected these gifts into a special box or drawer. The memories are etched into their souls, and they talk about what was said on that night as a fond memory.

At the end of the evening, a collective blessing was spoken to the honored son. Those present formed a circle and our son stood in the center. This circle around him symbolized the people in his life who are "for" him and not against him. The wonderful blessing of Numbers 6:24–26 was spoken:

> The LORD bless you
>    and keep you;
> the Lord make his face shine upon you
>    and be gracious to you;
> the Lord turn his face toward you
>    and give you peace.

Each celebration was filled with food, fun, tears, laughter, prayers, and meaningful conversation. Each of these rituals held all the ingredients of a soulful celebration that will be long remembered. Each offered the soulful gifts of honor, dignity, respect, and blessing to a beloved person. These are the sorts of gifts every soul needs.

## Your Soul Celebrations

1. How does celebrating a life passage minister to the soul?
2. What life passage could you celebrate for yourself?
3. What life passage could you celebrate for others?

# More Than a Meal

To eat is a necessity, but to eat intelligently is an art.

FRANÇOIS LA ROCHEFOUCAULD

"Let's have a feast and celebrate. For this son of mine was
dead and is alive again; he was lost and is found." So they
began to celebrate.

LUKE 15:23–24

Dinner with friends at a nice restaurant is a special occasion. We
choose inexpensive places that are quiet and where the service
is particularly good. The root word for *restaurant* comes through
French from the Latin word that means "restorer." When we enjoy a
good meal—including the food, drink, setting, and ambience—we
are restored.

When he was tempted by Satan (Matt. 4:4; Luke 4:4), Jesus quoted
Deuteronomy 8:3 that we live by the Word of God, not bread alone.
But it's also true that the physical body can't live long without bread.
The Christian novelist Frederick Buechner has said, "To eat is to ac-
knowledge our dependence—both on food and on each other. It also
reminds us of other kinds of emptiness that not even the Blue Plate
Special can touch."[1]

At one large conference there were meetings, talks, presentations,
and introductions to scores of people. But Gwen and I noticed that
the real sharing was at the dinner table. The sharing at meal times
was more than passing a plate of bread and butter; it was a soulful
sharing where lives touched each other as would be impossible at a
formal meeting. We were seated at intimate, round tables, where a

few people could sit, talk, and enter into each other's stories. At the table we unwrapped our feelings. We opened up to each other, and a sense of community and togetherness developed.

The expression "breaking bread together" is a beautiful reminder of what really happens when we gather around a table. When we break bread together, not only do we break the bread and share it as food, but we also share the events of our days. We can be together around the table as we can at no other time. Sharing a meal is one of the most effective things a family can do to promote connection and togetherness, but fast food and busy lives threaten this sacred gathering.

One of the best ways to practice soul care as a family or with friends is to have regular times of sharing a meal. The experience of sharing develops community around a table. I spoke to a college Christian group recently and was invited to an apartment to share in a "community meal" prior to our meeting. At this meal, several students share a simple bowl of soup and bread at someone's apartment. Each week different people are invited. Another college friend, Jacob, gets up on Sunday mornings to make pancakes for friends and "whoever else is hanging around." This is when a meal is more than a meal.

Jesus understood that a peaceful and joyful meal is associated with some of the greatest moments of our lives. It's amazing how often he is shown teaching in a meal setting (for example, Matt. 26:19–30; Mark 2:16–17; Luke 11:37; 14:1). At a table, Jesus made himself vulnerable to his friends; he described heaven in terms of the grandest banquet ever imagined (for example, Matt. 8:11; 22:2–14; Luke 22:29–30); it was at the wedding feast that Jesus performed a miracle of abundance (John 2:1–11); in the multiplication of loaves and fish Jesus demonstrated the ability of God to take care of the needs of his people (Matt. 14:14–21; 15:32–38 and parallels).

Every plate of food should remind us to bow and give thanks for what God has provided. Collectively, we express our hearts of gratitude to God for what we will share in a meal.

In the upper room a meal becomes the most dramatic expression of a meal's meaning. As the bread is broken and the cup is poured, the table becomes a place of worship, contemplation, and true sharing. It is high drama to watch the bread and cup being prepared (see Matt. 26:20–29; Mark 14:17–25; Luke 22:14–20), knowing that something important is about to happen. We are to come together regularly to the Lord's Table as a reminder of Christ's work and as nourishment for our souls.

A meal together is one of the most beautiful expressions of family or community life. Whether single or married, young or old, we take heart sitting at the same table, acknowledging that we are fellow travelers on the same journey.

### *Your Soul Celebrations*

1. What special meals do you remember from childhood?
2. What do you enjoy about a shared meal time?
3. How can a meal become more than a meal for you?

# 92

# Soulful Rituals

A commercial society whose members are essentially as-
cetic and indifferent in social ritual has to be provided
with blueprints and specifications for evoking the right
tone for every occasion.

MARSHALL MCLUHAN

And the child grew and became strong; he was filled with
wisdom, and the grace of God was upon him. Every year
his parents went to Jerusalem for the Feast of the Passover. When he was twelve years old, they went up to the
Feast, according to the custom.

LUKE 2:40–42

Rituals of the soul have been practiced by people of faith for thousands of years. The Bible is full of festivals, feasts, and times when
people gathered to remember, ask God's blessings, and acknowledge
the blessing of God upon their lives. Our challenge is to experience
the joy and depth of such times and also to make time for our souls.
Simple rituals help us create space for our souls to emerge and to
practice soul care.

Repeated actions that hold meaning and significance can be called
soulful rituals. Soulful rituals need not be elaborate or expensive.
They can be the "little things" of life that refresh and sustain us:

- lighting a candle at meal times;
- taking a walk before dinner;
- taking a nap on Sunday afternoons;

- sharing a meal with friends;
- practicing a quiet time each morning;
- praying in a specific place;
- engaging in physical exercise;
- reading a book before going to sleep;
- spending meaningful time each week with a friend;
- observing special days, times, and events; and
- listening to music at a certain time of the day.

Though often unaware of it, we practice rituals every day. The routine of getting ready for work or school combines necessary rituals like brushing our teeth and taking a shower. Soulful rituals renew our hearts. I like to sit alone early in the morning with a cup of freshly brewed coffee. I listen. I think. I pray. After I've finished my coffee, I pick up my Bible and read a psalm and part of another biblical book. Such a time helps prepare for the day's demands. When I travel I miss these quiet moments alone with God.

Simple rituals help define what we believe is important. Without them, we slide into soul atrophy and isolation, beliefs becomes fuzzy, we forget what is really important, and we can become cynical.

A simple ritual like playing favorite music after returning home or when friends visit can help soften the atmosphere and aid relaxation. Calling a friend on Sunday afternoons or writing a long overdue e-mail to a distant family member fosters love and connection.

Everyone can benefit from soulful rituals. Whatever the ritual, it needs to fit the shape of our individual and unique souls. Because when we care for our souls, we tend to what really matters.

### Your Soul Celebrations

1. What simple, routine pleasures do you enjoy?
2. How can you practice simple rituals?
3. How can you invite God to be a part of your daily routine?

# Notes

### Preface

1. See www.en.wikipedia.org/wiki/Impressionism (accessed February 17, 2005).

### Introduction

1. Daniel Taylor, *In Search of Sacred Places* (Saint Paul, MN: Bog Walk, 2005), 19.
2. Eugene Peterson's paraphrase of Jesus' words in Matthew 11:28–30 is the invitation to soul care. This is the invitation to discover Jesus in a whole new way.

### Chapter 1: Taking the Time

*Epigraph.* Quoted at Thinkexist.com, www.en.thinkexist.com/quotation/the_best_time_to_plant_a_tree_is_twenty_years_ago/254949 (accessed February 10, 2005). This popular folk proverb also is claimed in a slightly different form by Chinese Buddhists.

### Chapter 2: Soul Care 101

*Epigraph.* Richard Foster, *Celebration of Discipline: Path to Spiritual Growth* (New York: Harper Collins, 1978), 1.

1. See Stephen W. Smith, ed., *The Transformation of a Man's Heart* (Downers Grove, IL: InterVarsity, 2006), for discussion on authentic transformation and pseudotransformation. See also Stephen W. Smith, *Soul Shaping: A Practical Guide for Your Spiritual Transformation* (self-published; available through Potter's Inn).

## Chapter 3: The Inner Longing

*Epigraph.* Aleksandr Solzhenitsyn, quoted in Charles Colson, *Who Speaks for God? Confronting the World with Real Christianity* (Wheaton, IL: Crossway, 1985), 151.

1. Thomas Moore, *Care of the Soul* (New York: HarperCollins, 1992), xi.
2. Ibid.

## Chapter 4: The Ancient Path

*Epigraph.* John Newton, "A Sick Soul," in Olney Hymns, Vol. 1 (1779).

## Chapter 5: The Heart of the Matter

*Epigraph.* Brent Curtis and John Eldredge, *The Sacred Romance* (Nashville: Thomas Nelson, 1997), 3.

1. Emily E. S. Elliott, "Thou Didst Leave Thy Throne" (1864).

## Chapter 6: The Art of Curiosity

*Epigraph.* Barbara Brown Taylor, quoted at www.kleipotgemeente .typepad.com/soulgardeners/2003/01/ (accessed February 10, 2006).

## Chapter 7: Help Yourself First

*Epigraph.* Thomas à Kempis, *The Imitation of Christ*, trans. William C. Creasy (Notre Dame, IN: Ave Maria, 1989), 33.

## Chapter 8: The Beloved

*Epigraph.* Henri Nouwen, *Life of the Beloved: Spiritual Living in a Secular World* (New York: Crossroad, 1995), 28. I am grateful for Henri Nouwen's writings on "belovedness," particularly in *Life of the Beloved*. See also David Benner, *The Gift of Being Yourself: The Sacred Call to Self-Discovery* (Downers Grove, IL: InterVarsity, 2004), a wonderful resource for exploring our true identity as Christians.

1. Ibid.
2. Walter Trobisch, *Love Yourself* (Downers Grove, IL: InterVarsity, 1976), 19.

## Chapter 9: Soul Achievement

*Epigraph.* Quoted in Walter Trobish, *Love Yourself* (Downers Grove, IL: InterVarsity, 1976), 25–26.

1. Charlotte Elliott, "Just As I Am, Without One Plea" (1836).

## Chapter 10: The Turning Point

*Epigraph.* Quoted in Walter Trobisch, *Love Yourself* (Downers Grove, IL: InterVarsity, 1976), 9.

1. Ibid., 11.

## Chapter 11: The Divine Embrace

*Epigraph.* Ken Gire, *The Divine Embrace* (Carol Stream, IL: Tyndale, 2003), 61.

1. David Benner, *Surrender to Love* (Downers Grove, IL: InterVarsity, 2003), 16.

## Chapter 12: Soul Velcro

*Epigraph.* Philip Yancey, *What's So Amazing About Grace?* (Grand Rapids: Zondervan, 2002), 62.

## Chapter 13: Soulful Indulgence

*Epigraph.* Henri Nouwen, *In Joyful Hope: Meditations for Advent* (Creative Communications, 1997), 25.

## Chapter 14: Beloved Others

*Epigraph.* Henri Nouwen, *Life of the Beloved: Spiritual Living in a Secular World* (New York: Crossroad, 1995), 26.

## Chapter 15: Journey of the Soul

*Epigraph.* U2, "I Still Haven't Found What I'm Looking For," *The Joshua Tree*, compact disc (Island Records, 1987).

1. Augustine, *Confessions*, trans. Henry Chadwick (New York: Oxford University Press, 1991), 3.

## Chapter 16: Checking the Dipstick

*Epigraph.* Donald S. Whitney, *Simplify Your Spiritual Life* (Colorado Springs, CO: NavPress, 2003). From the Web page www.kleipotgemeente .typepad.com/soulgardeners/2003/01 (accessed February 10, 2006).

## Chapter 17: Embracing the Present

*Epigraph.* C. S. Lewis, *Mere Christianity* (New York: HarperCollins, 1980), 50.

## Chapter 18: Accepting the Past

*Epigraph.* Oswald Chambers, *My Utmost for His Highest* (New York: Dodd, Mead, 1935), December 31.

## Chapter 19: Relinquishing the Future

*Epigraph.* Quoted in Thinkexist.com, www.en.thinkexist.com/ quotation/the_best_thing_about_the_future_is_that_it_ comes/294249 (accessed February 10, 2006).

## Chapter 20: The Story of Exodus

*Epigraph.* Eugene Peterson, "Introduction to Exodus," *The Message* (Colorado Springs, CO: NavPress, 2002), 105.

1. Alister McGrath, *The Journey: A Pilgrim in the Lands of the Spirit* (New York: Doubleday, 2000), 23.

## Chapter 21: The Process of Endurance

*Epigraph.* Quoted in Creative Quotations, www.creativequotations .com/one/1603a (accessed February 10, 2006).

## Chapter 22: The Formative Years

*Epigraph.* Wayne Muller, *Legacy of the Heart* (New York: Fireside, 1992), xiv.

1. Lyle Dorsett, *Seeking the Secret Place: The Spiritual Formation of C. S. Lewis* (Grand Rapids: Brazos, 2004), 25.

## Chapter 23: Messy Work

*Epigraph.* Michael Yaconelli, *Messy Spirituality* (Grand Rapids: Zondervan, 2002), 10.

## Chapter 24: The Wake of Formation

*Epigraph.* Quoted in Quotations.com, www.quotations.home .worldnet.att.net/williamjames (accessed February 10, 2006).

## Chapter 25: The Misshapen Soul

*Epigraph.* Dorothy Corkille Briggs, *Your Child's Self Esteem: Step-by-Step Guidelines for Raising Responsible, Productive, Happy Children* (New York: Doubleday, 1975), 15.

## Chapter 26: Shaped by the Psalms

*Epigraph.* Eugene Peterson, "Introduction to Psalms," *The Message* (Colorado Springs, CO: NavPress, 2002), 911.

## Chapter 27: Grow Your Soul

*Epigraph.* Quoted in www.brainyquote.com/quotes/authors/m/ martin_luther_king_jr (accessed February 10, 2006). King was quoting Protestant Reformer Martin Luther.

1. This is the title of Eugene Peterson's wonderful book, *A Long Obedience in the Same Direction: Discipleship in an Instant Society* (Downers Grove, IL: InterVarsity, 1980).

## Chapter 28: Soul Hospitality

*Epigraph.* Benedict of Nursia, *The Rule of Saint Benedict in English*, ed. Timothy Fry (Collegeville, MN: Liturgical, 1981), 4:20.

## Chapter 29: The Need to Practice

*Epigraph.* Thomas Merton, *Thoughts on Solitude*, at www.watersedge .tv/disciplines_intro (accessed February 10, 2006).

1. For additional study on spiritual exercises, see Dallas Willard, *The Spirit of the Disciplines: Understanding How God Changes Lives* (San Francisco: HarperCollins, 1988).

## Chapter 30: Cries of the Soul

*Epigraph*. James Montgomery, "Prayer is the Soul's Sincere Desire" (1818). Originally a poem, this work was later set to music.

## Chapter 31: Soul Freedom

*Epigraph*. Evelyn Underhill, *The Spiritual Life* (1936), at www.mrrena .com/misc/sl (accessed February 10, 2006).

## Chapter 32: Sacred Reading

*Epigraph*. Henri Nouwen, *Bread for the Journey* (San Franciso: Harper-Collins, 1997), April 15.

## Chapter 33: The Joy of Confession

*Epigraph*. Augustine, in *Johannis evangelium* 12, 13: PL 35, 1491.
1. Keith Beasley-Topliffe, ed., *The Upper Room Dictionary of Christian Spiritual Formation* (Nashville: Upper Room Books, 2003), 65.

## Chapter 34: Listening for God

*Epigraph*. Benedict of Nursia, prologue to *The Rule of Saint Benedict in English*, ed. Timothy Fry (Collegeville, MN: Liturgical, 1981).
1. A. W. Tozer, *The Pursuit of God* (Harrisburg, PA: Christian Publications, 1982), 80.

## Chapter 35: Fasting from Life

*Epigraph*. Dallas Willard, *The Spirit of the Disciplines: Understanding How God Changes Lives* (reprint ed., San Francisco: HarperSanFrancisco, 1999).

## Chapter 36: Be Still and Know

*Epigraph*. Quoted in www.quotationsbook.com/quotes/10865/view (accessed February 11, 2006).

## Chapter 37: Necessary Solitudes

*Epigraph*. Lord Byron, *Childe Harold's Pilgrimage*, canto 3, stanza 90.

## Chapter 38: True Retreat

*Epigraph.* Dallas Willard, *The Spirit of the Disciplines: Understanding How God Changes Lives* (reprint ed., San Francisco: HarperSanFrancisco, 1999), 355.

## Chapter 39: Walking with God

*Epigraph.* Søren Kierkegaard, "Letter to Jette" (1847).

## Chapter 40: Holy Thinking

*Epigraph.* James Allen, "Effect of Thought on Circumstances," *As a Man Thinketh*, electronic version at www.concentric.net/~conure/allen02 (accessed February 20, 2006).

## Chapter 41: Journaling the Soul

*Epigraph.* Henry Blackaby and Claude V. King, *Experiencing God* (Nashville: Broadman & Holman, 1998), 172.

## Chapter 42: Sabbath Rest

*Epigraph.* Wayne Muller, *Sabbath: Finding Rest, Renewal, and Delight in Our Busy Lives* (New York: Bantam, 1999), 1.

1. Ibid.
2. Quoted in Erica Anderson, *The Schweitzer Album: A Portrait in Words and Pictures* (New York: Harper and Row, 1965).
3. Muller, *Sabbath*, 1.

## Chapter 43: Geography of the Soul

*Epigraph.* Augustine, *Confessions*, trans. Henry Chadwick (New York: Oxford University Press, 1991), 187.

## Chapter 44: Up the Mountain

*Epigraph.* John Muir, naturalist and writer. Quotation from a plaque in Yosemite National Park.

## Chapter 45: Sacred Waters

*Epigraph.* Quoted in www.americanrivers.org/site/PageServer?
pagename=AMR_content_09eb (accessed February 11, 2006).

## Chapter 46: In the Valley

*Epigraph.* G. K. Chesterton, *The Annotated Innocence of Father Brown:
A Detective Mystery* (reprint ed., Mineola, NY: Dover Publications,
1988), 194.

## Chapter 47: The Wilderness

*Epigraph.* Mary Jean Porter, *Sangre De Cristo Wilderness: A Territory of
the Heart* (Westcliffe, CO: Music Mountain, 1997), 16.

## Chapter 48: Desert Sanctuary

*Epigraph.* John C. Van Dyke, *The Desert* (1901), quoted at www
.utahredrocks.com/vandyke (accessed February 11, 2006).

## Chapter 49: Soul and the City

*Epigraph.* William Shakespeare, *Coriolanus*, act 3, scene 1.

## Chapter 50: Ministers to the Soul

*Epigraph.* Leonardo da Vinci, "Anatomy, Zoology, and Physiology,"
*The Notebooks of Leonardo da Vinci*, ed. Jean Paul Richter (1880). This
quotation is the title of essay 838.

## Chapter 51: The Glory of Sight

*Epigraph.* Quoted in Michael Garofalo, "Seeing, Vision, Perspective,"
at www.gardendigest.com/see (accessed February 21, 2006).

1. Ric Ergenbright, *The Art of God* (Wheaton, IL: Tyndale, 1999), 11.

## Chapter 52: The Wonder of Sound

*Epigraph.* Maltbie D. Babcock, "This Is My Father's World" (1901).

## Chapter 53: The Marvel of Touch

*Epigraph.* John Gillespie Magee Jr., "High Flight" (1942). "High Flight" was published after Pilot Officer Magee of the Royal Canadian Air Force was killed in a mid-air collision in the Battle for Britain, December 11, 1941.

### Chapter 54: The Goodness of Taste

*Epigraph.* Quoted in Food Reference Web site www.foodreference .com/html/qsoulfood (accessed February 21, 2006).

### Chapter 55: The Scent of the Sacred

*Epigraph.* Quoted in "Helen Keller," at www.cybernation.com/ quotationcenter/quoteshow.php?type=author&id=4828 (accessed February 21, 2006).

### Chapter 56: The Power of Imagination

*Epigraph.* Quoted in www.earlychristianwritings.com/Ignatius (accessed March 10, 2006).

### Chapter 57: An Extreme Makeover

*Epigraph.* Quoted in R. Buckminster Fuller Web site, www .fusionanomaly.net/rbuckminsterfuller (accessed February 20, 2006).

1. For information about authentic transformation and pseudotransformation, see Stephen W. Smith, *Soul Shaping: A Practical Guide for Your Spiritual Transformation* (available through Potter's Inn).

### Chapter 58: Soulful Addictions

*Epigraph.* Quoted in www.brainyquote.com/quotes/quotes/k/ kenhensley230254 (accessed March 10, 2006).

### Chapter 59: Confessions of a Workaholic

*Epigraph.* Quoted in "Tools for Recovery" at www.royy.com/ toolsofrecovery (accessed March 10, 2006).

### Chapter 60: Sins of the Soul

*Epigraph.* John Newton, "Physician of My Sin-Sick Soul," *Olney Hymns,* vol. 1 (1779).

1. Karl Menninger, *Whatever Became of Sin?* (New York: Hawthorn, 1973).

## Chapter 61: Soul and Body

*Epigraph.* Oswald Chambers, *My Utmost for His Highest* (New York: Dodd Mead & Co., 1935), August 9.

## Chapter 62: Soul Carnage

*Epigraph.* David Whyte, *Crossing the Unknown Sea: Work as a Pilgrimage of Identity* (New York: Penguin, 2002).

## Chapter 63: Satan and the Soul

*Epigraph.* Quoted in www.aquarionics.com/assets/quoth/wisdom.quotes (accessed March 1, 2006).

## Chapter 64: SALVE for the Soul

*Epigraph.* Charles Haddon Spurgeon, "The Minister's Fainting Fits," lecture 11 in *Lectures to My Students* (reprint ed., Grand Rapids: Zondervan, 1972).

1. E. B. White, *Charlotte's Web* (New York: HarperCollins, 1952), 11.
2. John Powell, S.J., *Why Am I Afraid to Tell You Who I Am?* (Chicago: Thomas More Association, 1990).
3. See J. B. Calvert, "How Geysers Work" at the University of Denver Web site, www.du.edu/~jcalvert/geol/geyser (accessed February 20, 2006).

## Chapter 65: Marred Souls

*Epigraph.* Quoted in www.daily-motivational-quote.com/motivationalquote (accessed March 10, 2006).

## Chapter 66: Disappointed Souls

*Epigraph.* Quoted in "Henry David Thoreau," www.en.proverbia.net/citasautor.asp?autor=17230&page=10 (accessed February 20, 2006).

## Chapter 67: The Stressed Soul

*Epigraph.* Quoted in "Motivational and Inspirational quotes," Motivational and Inspirational Corner: America's System for Success Web site, at www.motivational-inspirational-corner.com/getquote .html?categoryid=134.

## Chapter 68: The Anatomy of Discouragement

*Epigraph.* Quoted in Clayton E. Tucker-Ladd, *Psychological Self-Help* (electronic self-published book, Tucker-Ladd and the Self-Help Foundation, 2005), 525.

## Chapter 69: The Aroma of Failure

*Epigraph.* Quoted in "Lite Side," in *The Lutheran*, November 2000.

## Chapter 70: When You Feel Broadsided

*Epigraph.* William Shakespeare, *Hamlet*, act 5, scene 2.

## Chapter 71: The Furnace of Transformation

*Epigraph.* From the ancient collection of stories and quotations of the desert fathers, *Paradise of the Fathers*, trans. from Syriac by A. E. Budge (various editions).

## Chapter 72: Cocooning Toward Change

*Epigraph.* Trina Paulus, *Hope for the Flowers*, 25th anniversary ed. (Mahwah, NJ: Paulist, 1997).

## Chapter 73: The Meaning of Companionship

*Epigraph.* Alan Jones, *Exploring Spiritual Direction: An Essay on Christian Friendship* (New York: Seabury, 1982), 30.

1. "Miner Miracle," *The Gazette*, Colorado Springs, July 29, 2002.

## Chapter 74: The Heart of Companionship

*Epigraph.* Quoted in Dorothy Riera, "Literary Thoughts on Friendship," www.spirituality.org/is/007/page06 (accessed February 20, 2006).

## Chapter 75: The Lost Art of Having a Buddy

*Epigraph.* Quoted in Bella Online quotations collection for women, www.bellaonline.com/articles/art16802 (accessed February 20, 2006).

1. John Donne, "Meditation 17," *Devotions Upon Emergent Occasions* (1624).
2. Nancy Geffrey, "Whatever Happened to Friendship?" *Wall Street Journal*, March 3, 2000.

## Chapter 76: A Soulful Advocate

*Epigraph.* Quoted in www.studyworld.com/newsite/quotes/QuoteByTopic.asp?i=Friendship (accessed March 7, 2006).

1. Eugene Peterson, *Leap over a Wall: Earthly Spirituality for Everyday Christians* (San Francisco: HarperCollins, 1997), 54.

## Chapter 77: About Intimacy

*Epigraph.* C. S. Lewis, *The Four Loves: Essays on Affection, Friendship, Erotic Love, and Charity* (London: G. Bles, 1960), 113.

## Chapter 78: Archiving and Forgiveness

*Epigraph.* Henri Nouwen, *Bread for the Journey* (San Francisco: HarperCollins, 1997), January 26.

1. Ibid.

## Chapter 79: Souls in Community

*Epigraph.* Dietrich Bonhoeffer, *Life Together,* trans. John W. Doberstein (New York: Harper & Brothers, 1954), 77.

## Chapter 80: The Elusive Nature of Success

*Epigraph.* Tom Morris, interview by Anna Muoio, "The Philosopher," *Fast Company* 26 (July 1999): 140.

1. Ibid.

## Chapter 81: Soul Care and Money

*Epigraph*. Quoted in www.dailychristianquote.com, February 6, 2002.

## Chapter 82: Who Defines You?

*Epigraph*. Søren Kierkegaard, *The Prayers of Kierkegaard*, ed. Perry LeFevre (Chicago: University of Chicago Press, 1956), 147.

*Epigraph*. Walter Trobisch, *Love Yourself: Self-Acceptance and Depression* (Downers Grove, IL: InterVarsity, 1976).

1. Quoted in David G. Benner, *The Gift of Being Yourself* (Downers Grove, IL: InterVarsity, 2004), 20.
2. John Calvin, *Institutes of the Christian Religion,* trans. Ford Lewis Battles, 1536 ed. (Grand Rapids: Eerdmans, 1995), 15.
3. Walter Trobisch, *Love Yourself* (Downers Grove, IL: InterVarsity, 1976), 19.

## Chapter 83: Desires of the Soul

*Epigraph*. Blaise Pascal, *Pensees*, section 6.

## Chapter 84: The Power of the Dash

*Epigraph*. Attributed to Scottish national hero William Wallace in the screenplay by Randall Wallace, *Braveheart* (Writers Guild of America, 1995).

## Chapter 85: Leaving a Legacy of Faith

*Epigraph*. Quoted by Stephanie Tubbs Jones in the keynote address, Martin Luther King Jr. Day convocation, Case Western Reserve University, January 30, 1997.

## Chapter 86: Holes in the Soul

*Epigraph*. George Herbert, *Outlandish Proverbs* (1640).

## Chapter 87: Soulful Celebrations

*Epigraph*. This motivational business speaker and writer is quoted in www.cybernation.com/quotationcenter/quoteshow.

## Chapter 88: The Blessing of the Soul

*Epigraph*. George Eliot (Mary Ann Evans Cross), *Janet's Repentance* (1857), 68. See at Classiq.net Digital Library, www.classiq.net/george-eliot/janets-repentance/page-67 (accessed February 20, 2006).

1. Henri Nouwen, *Life of the Beloved: Spiritual Living in a Secular World* (New York: Crossroad, 1995), 56.

## Chapter 89: A Birthday for the Soul

*Epigraph*. Robert Browning, "Rabbi Ben Ezra" (1864), line 1.

## Chapter 90: Soul Passage

*Epigraph*. James Taylor, "Secret o' Life," *Jt*, compact disc (Sony, 2000).

## Chapter 91: More Than a Meal

*Epigraph*. François La Rochefoucauld, *Sentences and Moral Maxims* (1665). La Rochefoucauld (1613–1680) was a seventeenth-century essayist and social critic of the French court, who was imprisoned and banished for his reform efforts against Cardinal Richelieu. His comment on eating is frequently used by gourmets, but it was originally from a satire on the eating habits of the nobility.

1. Frederick Buechner, *Wishful Thinking* (San Francisco: Harper, 1973), 13.

## Chapter 92: Soulful Rituals

*Epigraph*. Marshall McLuhan, "Emily Post," *The Mechanical Bride: Folklore of Industrial Man* (1951; reprint ed., Boston: Beacon, 1968).

# About the Potter's Inn Ministry

The Potter's Inn is dedicated to the work of Christian spiritual formation through its ministry and retreat center. Founders Stephen W. and Gwen H. Smith offer guided retreats, individual help, and resources that explore spiritual transformation. The Smiths also travel throughout the United States and to other countries, conducting seminars and guiding individuals who long for deeper intimacy with God.

Through creative retreats, speaking, writing, and sharing, Steve and Gwen have helped many people experience the transformation of the Potter's hands.

Much of this work is done at Potter's Inn at Aspen Ridge, a retreat center located on a ranch in Divide, Colorado. This retreat center, with its refurbished log cabins, trails, and magnificent views of the Colorado Rockies is available for soul care, retreats, and vacations. Guided retreats are offered throughout the year in Colorado and at various places around the world. Soul care is available at the Potter's Inn through weekly sessions or by coming for a week or two and utilizing the cabins and retreat facilities. Soul Care Intensives are offered for leaders who need a time of renewal, direction, and restoration.

As frequent speakers and retreat leaders, Steve and Gwen have committed themselves to the spiritual growth and transformation of individuals, couples, churches, and organizations. Steve's writings and small-group guides are key components of the Potter's Inn Ministry. Steve has spoken in churches in North America, Europe, Africa, and Haiti. He frequently addresses student groups on college campuses through InterVarsity, Campus Crusade, and Athletes in Action. He is also a former adjunct professor of preaching at Tyndale Theological Seminary in Badhovedorp, the Netherlands, and is currently an adjunct teacher at Missionary Training International in Monument, Colorado.

The Smiths have been involved in Christian ministry since 1979. Steve studied at Lenoir Rhyne College, Southern Baptist Theological Seminary, and Trinity Evangelical Divinity School. In their pioneering work, they planted and pastored churches in North America and Europe.

While in Europe, Steve ministered behind the iron curtain in churches in Poland, the former East Germany, and Romania. In Poland and Romania he helped to foster partnership churches to aid in smuggling Bibles and food to hungry Christians.

**Other Potter's Inn resources and books:**

The Beloved Ring™ is individually crafted and made of sterling silver. A beautiful gift of honor and distinction. Available in men's and women's sizes. "Beloved" is etched twice on the ring. A lasting gift of memory and honor to the Beloved!

The Forming Hands Pendant is individually crafted and made of sterling silver. Suitable for necklace or charm. Measures 5/8" in height. A gift to thank the hands that shaped and formed you!

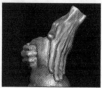

The Forming Hands Sculpture reveals the two dramatic and unique hands of the Divine Potter. A meaningful gift for a pastor, teacher, coach, parent, or mentor. Made of resin. Comes with booklet.

Smith, Stephen W. *Soul Shaping: A Practical Guide for Your Spiritual Transformation.* Colorado Springs, CO: Potter's Inn, 2005.

Smith, Stephen W., ed. *The Transformation of a Man's Heart.* Downers Grove, IL: InterVarsity Press, 2006. Contributors include Fil Anderson, Howard Baker, David Benner, Ross Campbell, Gary Chapman, Gordon Dalbey, Craig Glass, John Pierce, Stephen W. Smith, Doug Stewart.

Smith, Stephen W., ed. *The Transformation of a Man's Heart Series: Transformation, Sex, Marriage, and Work.* Downers Grove, IL: InterVarsity Press, 2006. Six sessions in each guide for individual or group use.

**For more information contact:**

> Potter's Inn
> 6660 Delmonico Drive, Suite D-180
> Colorado Springs, CO 80919
> Telephone: 719-264-8837
> Web site: www.pottersinn.com
> e-mail: resources@pottersinn.com

If your have enjoyed this book and are interested in
learning more about caring for your soul, e-mail
embracingsoulcare@kregel.com.